BLUE-RIBBON PIES

ALSO BY MARIA POLUSHKIN ROBBINS

The Dumpling Cookbook
The Cook's Quotation Book
Blue-Ribbon Pickles & Preserves

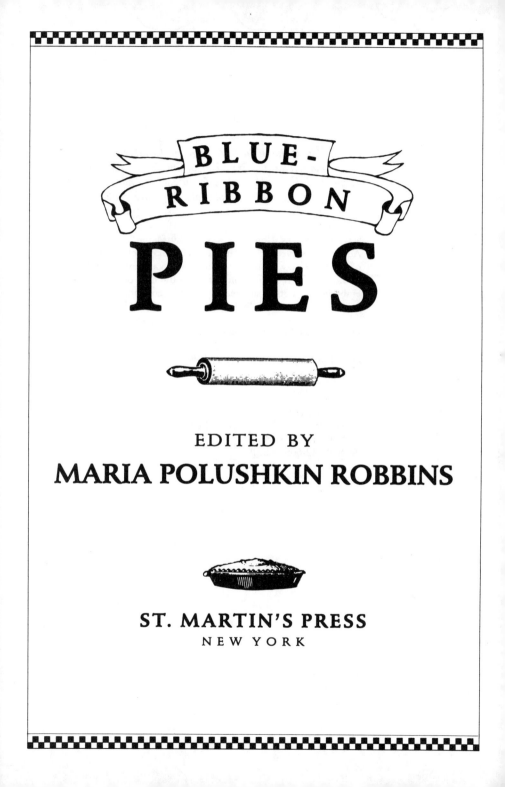

BLUE-RIBBON
PIES

EDITED BY
MARIA POLUSHKIN ROBBINS

ST. MARTIN'S PRESS
NEW YORK

I would like to thank the Anchorage Fur Rendezvous, the Los Angeles County Fair, the State Fair of Oklahoma, the State Fair of Texas, and the Michigan 4-H Foundation for allowing me to reprint recipes from cookbooks they have published.

Design by Claire B. Counihan

Library of Congress Cataloging-in-Publication Data

Robbins, Maria Polushkin.
   Blue-ribbon pies.

   1. Pastry   1. Title.
TX773.P65   1987   641.8'652   87-1700
ISBN 0-312-00732-9/HC
ISBN 0-312-00569-5/PB

10   9   8   7   6   5

Contents

THE PIES (*cont.*)

Acknowledgments

Though I worked alone on this project, I was, by mail and phone, connected with hundreds of people all over the country. If I sent out so many letters that the local postal clerk groaned when he saw me coming, I received so many responses that my mailman was positively staggered by the load. This is *truly* a book that would not have happened without tons of generous help—from the officers of the state and regional fair organizations who waded through their records to send me the names and addresses of their prizewinning cooks; and, of course, most of all from the cooks themselves who shared their recipes with me and readers of this book. My heartfelt thanks to them all. Thanks, too, to Jim Charlton, Barbara Binswanger, and Cara De Silva, who cooked up the idea for this project; to Barbara Anderson, my editor, who was patient and helpful; and finally to my husband, Ken, who helped stuff and seal all those envelopes.

BLUE-RIBBON PIES

Introduction

"As American as . . ." No one can see that phrase without thinking of apple pie, as, indeed, no one can think of that most American of American institutions—the country fair—without thinking of prizewinning pies. And not just apple pie, but blueberry and peach, rhubarb, lemon meringue, and chocolate or coconut cream; deep dish or not, covered or open. And the combinations: strawberry-rhubarb, blueberry-peach, honey raisin pear. The possibilities go on endlessly, which explains, perhaps, why the pie table always seems to be the center of attention at any fair. A pie is such a simple thing, and perfect in its simplicity, and yet it's the variety, the limitlessly personalized possibilities of the pie that make it the object of such interest and the subject of such pride.

At a time when food tastes are being dictated by trendy experts, it's comforting to know that Americans are still making pies the way they always did, often from recipes handed down from mother to daughter (or, increasingly, from father to son) for generations. Of course, you won't find them at the trendy restaurants, and you won't find them offered at any of the fast-food chains. No, if you want an old-fashioned sort of pie, the genuine article, you're going to have to check out the church socials and the county, regional, and state fairs of America, and that is exactly what I did for this book.

I wrote to every organized fair listed in the I.A.F.E. (International Association of Fairs and Expositions) Directory asking for the names and addresses of their current prizewinners. Then I wrote to the winners and asked them for their pie recipes. I expected a little resistance—after all, many of

these recipes have been closely guarded family se-
crets for who knows how long. But the response
was overwhelmingly generous. Hundreds of recipes were submitted from all over the country, and
my only problem (a delicious one) was deciding on
the final selection.

These recipes represent the best work of America's amateur regional cooks, judged not by na-
tional food critics or editors but by their friends and
neighbors. I hope you enjoy them.

Tips for Making Perfect Pie Crusts

The basic ingredients of pastry pie crusts are simple: flour, fat, water, and salt. The type of fat or shortening used will affect the flavor and texture of the crust. Lard or solid vegetable shortening make for a flaky, tender texture. Butter imparts a delicate flavor, but used alone will give a hard crisp texture. A blend of lard or solid vegetable shortening and butter makes a tasty and tender combination. Occasionally oil is called for in a recipe. Oil crust pies are easy to make because the crust is usually pressed right into the pie pan, instead of being rolled out. Oil gives the crust a mealy rather than flaky texture, and makes a perfect crust for liquid fillings.

Optional ingredients include eggs, sugar, vinegar, a leavening such as baking powder, and flavorings. An egg can add extra crispness and a rich taste. Sugar is added for sweetness and a darker color. Vinegar can provide an extra dimension of tenderness. Leavening is used to provide lightness. A flavoring such as grated orange or lemon peel, vanilla, or chocolate provides variety and interest.

A second type of pie crust isn't made from pastry at all but from crumbs of crackers or cookies—most commonly graham crackers. The crumbs are mixed with melted butter, sugar, and other flavorings and pressed into a pie plate.

Part of the fun of making pies is experimenting with different types of crusts in combination with different kinds of fillings. Some of the recipes in this book specify a particular combination of pie crust and filling, and that fact is indicated in the specific recipes; some, however, simply call for a single- or double-crust pie shell. In any case, you

can feel free to make your own selection of pie pastry from the recipes in the section on crusts. Soon enough you will have your own favorite recipes to pass on to your children and grandchildren.

The following instructions are for making pie crust by hand. Most pie crusts can be made in a food processor as well, but for best results you should follow the manufacturer's instructions.

Mixing Pie Pastry

- Use all-purpose flour.
- Keep cool. A cool room, a cool work surface, and cool utensils and ingredients all help make it easier to produce a flaky, tender crust.
- For very flaky pastry, chill shortening for 15 to 20 minutes in the freezer before using.
- Combine dry ingredients first.
- Cut in shortening with a pastry blender or two knives used scissor fashion. For a flaky crust, distribute the fat as evenly as possible. The mixture should resemble tiny peas or a coarse meal. Work quickly and do not overwork the mixture or the shortening will become soft and sticky. This will make a tough, hard crust.
- Use the coldest possible water to keep fat particles solid.
- Sprinkle water over flour mixture a little at a time and toss with a fork to distribute well. Use only enough water to make pastry hold together. Flour mixture should feel moist, not wet.
- Gather dough into a ball. Do not knead the dough. Pie pastry should be handled as little as possible. Divide into balls according to recipe.
- Let it rest. Almost all pie pastry benefits from a rest in the refrigerator—from 30 minutes to 24 hours. This step alone can eliminate many problems. A cool rest tenderizes the pastry, makes it

easier to roll out, and keeps pastry from getting soggy.

Rolling Out Pastry
- Remove pastry dough from refrigerator about 20 minutes before rolling out for easier rolling.
- A well-floured pastry cloth or a lightly floured board are ideal nonstick surfaces for rolling out pie pastry.
- A well-floured stockinette (a knitted cotton stocking made to fit over a rolling pin, available in cookware departments everywhere) over your rolling pin will help roll out pie dough easier and faster.
- Flatten the cold pastry dough lightly into a small circle, then use rolling pin to roll out a circle that is 3 inches larger in diameter than the pie pan you plan to use. The dough should be approximately ⅛ inch thick.
- Always roll from the middle of dough out, using short quick strokes and lifting rolling pin as it comes to the edge. This prevents edges from getting too thin.
- Lift the pastry from time to time to make sure that it isn't sticking. If it is sticking, loosen with a spatula and sprinkle a little flour on the surface underneath.
- If there is a crack or break in the pastry, patch it with a little strip of pastry cut from the edge. Moisten the patch, press into place, and continue rolling out.
- Work quickly so pastry dough does not get soft and sticky.

Lining the Pie Plate
- Do not grease pie pans before lining with pastry.
- To move rolled pastry dough to a pie plate, drape dough loosely around rolling pin, then unroll onto

plate. Alternatively, fold pastry dough in half, place fold in center of pie plate, and unfold.

- Gently ease the dough onto bottom and sides of pie plate. Do not stretch or pull but leave a loose fit. Pastry will shrink while baking. Use fingers to pat pastry gently into place to eliminate any air pockets.

- *For a single-crust pie:* Trim the pastry with kitchen shears so it is just about even with the edges of the pie pan or just a little bit larger. Make a fluted edge by pinching the edges of the dough with your thumb and forefinger. Or simply press the edges all around with the tines of a fork.

- *For a double-crust pie:* Do not trim overhang of pastry in pie plate. Roll out top pastry dough as for bottom crust, so that it is ⅛ inch thick and about 1 inch larger around than the pie plate. Use a sharp knife to cut steam slits, or prick all over with the tines of a fork. Alternatively, steam vents may be cut after the top crust is placed on the pie. Drape pastry onto rolling pin and place it over the filled pie shell. Trim both crusts all around, leaving approximately ½- to 1-inch overhang. Pinch edges together with fingers to make a fluted edge, or crimp all around with the tines of a fork.

- *For a lattice top:* Trim the edges of the bottom crust, leaving a 1-inch overhang. Fill the pie shell. Roll pastry for top crust into a circle approximately ⅛ inch thick. Cut the pastry into ½-inch strips. Brush the edges of the bottom crust with water. Place pastry strips about 1 inch apart across the pie. Press strips at both ends to seal. Repeat with an equal number of pastry strips placed at right angles to the first ones. Turn overhang up over pastry strips and make a fluted edge.

Baking the Pie

■ Know your oven! Everybody's oven is different, no matter what manufacturers say. Use the temperatures and baking times given in each recipe as a guideline, but be governed by your own observations and experience.

■ Bake pies in middle of the oven for even heat.

■ Preheat oven for a full 15 minutes before baking.

■ If crust or edges of crust are browning too fast, cover lightly with aluminum foil and continue baking until done.

■ *To bake an unfilled pie shell:* Prick dough evenly with the tines of a fork. Line the bottom crust with buttered aluminum foil, place buttered side down. Fill with dried beans or rice. (These may be saved and re-used for the same purpose.) Remove beans or rice and foil for last 5 minutes of baking to brown the crust fully. Some pie crusts may be baked without the foil and rice or beans. Follow instructions for individual recipe.

Freezing Pastry and Unbaked Pie Shells

■ Wrap balls of pastry dough tight in plastic and freezer paper, label, and freeze for up to 2 months. Thaw at room temperature for 2 to 4 hours.

■ Another way to freeze pastry dough is to roll it out into circles and stack it with wax paper between each circle. Wrap well and freeze. To use, place dough circle on pie plate and thaw for 15 to 20 minutes at room temperature before using.

■ Freeze unbaked pie shells in pie plates. Wrap well and freeze for up to 2 months. No need to thaw before baking.

Miscellaneous Tips

■ When making meringue, have all ingredients at room temperature.

■ Custard fillings that are precooked should be beaten until they are cool to allow steam to escape before they are turned into a pie shell. Otherwise steam will condense and make filling watery.

- Cool pies on a rack. Air circulates and pie cools faster. Even pies that are to be served warm should cool slightly when they come out of the oven and be given some time to pull themselves together.
- Relax and enjoy your pies!

THE PIE CRUSTS

Basic Pie Crust

For 1 single-crust, 8- or 9-inch pie:
1 cup all-purpose flour
½ teaspoon salt
⅓ cup plus 1 tablespoon shortening*
2 tablespoons cold water

For 1 double-crust, 8- or 9-inch pie:
1½ cups all-purpose flour
¾ teaspoon salt
½ cup plus 2 tablespoons shortening*
3 tablespoons water

*If lard is used, reduce shortening to ⅓ cup for one crust and ½ cup for two crusts.

Mix together flour and salt. Cut in shortening until particles are the size of tiny peas. Sprinkle on water a tablespoon at a time. Mix only enough for dough to come away from sides of bowl. Form into ball(s). This dough does not require chilling, although it may rest in refrigerator until needed.

Roll out pastry and ease into pie pan. If you are making a double-crust pie, roll out top crust.

To bake before filling:
Preheat oven to 425° F.
Prick bottom of dough evenly with tines of fork. Cover the dough with buttered foil, placing buttered side against the bottom crust. Fill with rice or beans. These may be saved and used again for baking unfilled pie shells. Bake for 15 minutes, or until set. Remove foil, and bake 5 minutes longer, or until golden. Let cool before filling.

Carol Sisler
Orleans, Michigan
Ionia County
Free Fair

Mostly Butter Pie Crust

For 1 double-crust, 9-inch pie, or 2 single-crust pies:

1¾ cups flour
10 tablespoons butter, chilled
3 tablespoons shortening, chilled
½ cup ice water
1 egg, beaten

Blend flour, butter, and shortening until mixture resembles coarse meal. Add a little water, and mix until dough just starts to come together. Gather into ball and divide in half. Shape each half into a ball, flour lightly, and wrap in plastic. If you are making one single-crust pie, freeze one ball of pastry for another time. Chill the pastry you are using for 2 hours.

Roll out pastry and ease into a 9-inch pie pan. If you are making a double-crust pie, roll out top crust.

To bake before filling:

Preheat oven to 425°F.

Prick the bottom of dough evenly all over with the tines of a fork. Cover the dough with buttered foil, placing buttered side against the bottom crust. Fill with rice or beans. These may be saved and used again for baking unfilled pie shells. Bake for 15 minutes, or until set. Remove foil, brush with egg, and bake 5 minutes longer, or until golden. Let cool before filling.

Jaymi Sandler
Anchorage, Alaska
Anchorage Fur
Rendezvous

Margarine Pastry

Pie pastry made with margarine is easy to work and gives a smooth, firm, yellow-colored crust. Stick margarine will give better results than soft margarine.

Many cooks sift their flour before measuring. Mrs. Teichman prefers to spoon her flour into the measuring cup.

For 1 double-crust, 10-inch pie, or 2 single-crust pies:

2 cups lightly spooned flour
1 teaspoon salt
1 tablespoon sugar
12 tablespoons margarine
¼ cup cold water

Sift together flour, salt, and sugar. Cut half the mixture into the flour with a pastry blender or two table knives till the mixture resembles cornmeal. Cut the rest of the margarine into this mixture until it resembles small peas. This makes a flakier crust. Sprinkle the mixture with water, adding enough extra to make pastry hold together. Use a pastry blender or fork because the heat of your hands will tend to melt the margarine. Mix just to moisten, and form into a ball. Let stand in the refrigerator for a few minutes while you prepare the pie filling ingredients. Or wrap in plastic and chill several hours or overnight.

Rolling out:

Divide the dough in half. Roll bottom crust on a lightly floured pastry cloth. Roll out at least 1 inch wider than pie pan. If crust breaks, gently pinch together with fingers. Always roll from center outward. Place in pie pan.

Mrs. Colleen K.
Teichman
Kalispell, Montana
Northwest
Montana Fair

Pie Crust with Margarine and Lard

For 1 double-crust, 10-inch pie, or 2 single-crust pies:

2½ cups sifted flour
½ teaspoon salt
¼ pound lard
6 tablespoons margarine
¼ cup ice water

Sift together flour and salt. Cut lard and margarine into flour mixture until crumbs are the size of small peas. Add ice water a little at a time and toss with a fork. Form into ball and divide in half. Let rest in refrigerator, if desired. Roll out two circles on a lightly floured board to fit a 10-inch pie pan.

Sister Concepta
Marie Nudo
Peoria, Illinois
Heart of Illinois Fair

Crisco Pie Crust

For 2 double-crust, 9-inch pies, or 4 single-crust pies:

4 cups sifted flour
1 teaspoon baking powder
2 teaspoons salt
2 tablespoons sugar
1½ cups Crisco
1 egg
1 teaspoon vinegar
½ cup cold water

Sift flour, baking powder, salt, and sugar together in a bowl. Cut in shortening and blend. Beat egg, vinegar, and water together and work into flour mixture. Roll pastry into a ball and divide into four equal parts. If you are making one double-crust pie, wrap two balls of pastry in plastic and freeze for a future pie.

For baked shell and lattice:

(Called for in the recipe for Blueberry-Peach Pie, page 46.) Preheat oven to 450°F. Roll out one pastry ball and place in a 9-inch pie plate. Flute edges. Prick bottom with a fork. Roll out the other pastry ball and cut into lattice strips for top. Place them on cookie sheet. Bake pie shell for 10 to 12 minutes, until golden brown. Bake lattice strips for 5 to 8 minutes. Let cool before filling.

Arleen Owen
Fresno, California
Fresno Fair

Never-Fail Pie Crust

For 2 double-crust, 9-inch pies:

1¼ cups shortening
3 cups flour
1 teaspoon salt
1 egg, beaten
5 tablespoons water
1 tablespoon vinegar

Cut shortening into flour and salt. Combine egg, water, and vinegar. Pour liquid into flour mixture all at once. Blend until all is moistened. Roll into four equal balls, wrap in plastic, and refrigerate until ready to use. Keeps in refrigerator for up to 2 weeks.

Bonnie Read
Naples, Florida
Collier County Fair

Oil Pie Crust

This makes a tender, flaky crust. The pastry needs no rest or refrigeration. Well wrapped, it will keep in the refrigerator for several days.

For 2 double-crust, 9-inch pies plus 1 single-crust pie:

4½ cups flour
1½ cups Crisco oil
1 teaspoon salt
½ cup ice-cold water

With a fork, blend flour, oil, and salt in a large bowl. Add water a little at a time and blend in with the fork. Continue until pastry holds together. Divide into five equal parts. Roll into balls. Store in refrigerator or freezer until needed.

Linda Hebert
Louisville, Kentucky
Southeast
Washington
State Fair
Walla Walla,
Washington

Boiling Water Pastry

An easy-to-make crust with a solid texture that is well suited for soft fillings.

For 3 single-crust, 9-inch pies, or 1 double-crust, 9-inch pie plus 1 single-crust, 9-inch pie:

½ cup boiling water
1 cup shortening
3 cups flour
½ teaspoon salt
½ teaspoon baking powder

Add the boiling water to the shortening. Beat until creamy and thick. Sift flour, salt, and baking powder together and stir into creamed mixture. Mix well and refrigerate for several hours before rolling out.

Mrs. Katie Gilbert
Germanton,
North Carolina
Dixie Classic Fair

All-Purpose Pie Crust Made with Lard

Serious pie makers have always known that lard makes the flakiest crust.

For 3 double-crust, 9-inch pies:

6 cups flour
3 teaspoons salt
1 pound lard
1 egg, beaten
2 scant tablespoons cider vinegar
Cold water

Measure flour and salt into a large bowl. Cut lard into small pieces and drop into flour. Blend with a pastry blender or two knives until mixture resembles coarse crumbs. (This mixture may be stored in a plastic bag or other airtight container in the refrigerator almost indefinitely.)

Combine beaten egg with vinegar in a 1-cup measuring cup, and add cold water to make 1 cup of liquid. Mix liquid with flour mixture just until pastry holds together, then divide into six balls of dough. Two balls make 1 double-crust, 9-inch pie. Wrap balls in plastic and refrigerate for several hours before rolling out, or freeze for future use.

For 1 double-crust, 9-inch pie:

1 beaten egg
2 teaspoons cider vinegar
2 heaping cups of flour mixture
Cold water as necessary

Mix egg with cider vinegar, then combine with flour mixture. Add just enough water for pastry to hold together. Form into a ball, divide in half, and roll out.

Patricia Boyden
Mt. Morris,
Michigan
Genesee
County Fair

Pastry Mix
for Pie Crust

If you enjoy making pies as much as Norma Fenn, you'll want to have her time-saving pastry mix at the ready in your refrigerator. It will keep for up to a month.

For 8½ cups pastry mix:

7 cups sifted all-purpose flour
4 teaspoons salt
1 pound (about 2 cups) lard, chilled
or
1 pound (about 2½ cups) other shortening, chilled

Mix flour and salt thoroughly; cut in cold shortening until particles are no larger than small peas. Store in tightly sealed container and refrigerate.

For 1 single-crust, 9-inch pie:

1½ cups pastry mix
2 to 3 tablespoons cold water

Mix lightly, form into a ball, and roll out.

For 1 double-crust, 9-inch pie:

2½ cups pastry mix
4 to 6 tablespoons cold water

Mix lightly, form into a ball, divide in two, and roll out.

Norma Fenn
Roseburg, Oregon
Douglas
County Fair

Orange-Flavored Pastry

For 1 single-crust, 9-inch pie with lattice top:

1½ cups unbleached flour
1 tablespoon grated orange peel
½ teaspoon salt
½ cup shortening
2 tablespoons orange juice
2 to 3 tablespoons water

In a medium bowl, combine flour, orange peel, and salt. Using a pastry blender, cut in shortening until mixture resembles coarse crumbs. Sprinkle orange juice and water, 1 tablespoon at a time, over flour mixture, while tossing and mixing lightly with a fork. Add liquid until dough is just moist enough to hold together.

Shape dough into two balls, one twice the size of the other. Roll larger ball on a floured surface into a circle 1½ inches larger than 9-inch pie pan. Fold dough in half and unfold into pan. Do not stretch. Trim ½ inch beyond pan edge. Roll out smaller ball and cut into strips for lattice top.

Ron Stanford
South Gate,
California
L.A. County Fair

Sugar Pie Crust

A delicious pie crust to bake first and fill later, especially with fruit.

For 1 single-crust baked pie shell:

1 heaping cup flour
3½ tablespoons confectioners' sugar
¼ pound butter

Preheat oven to 350°F.

Combine flour and confectioners' sugar. Cut in butter and blend to a pie dough consistency. Press the dough evenly into an 8- or 9-inch pie plate. Prick dough all over bottom with the tines of a fork. Bake for 20 minutes, until lightly browned. Remove and let cool.

Jane E. Hurshma
Springfield, Illinois
Illinois State Fair

Nutty Chocolate Pie Dough

For 1 single-crust, baked 9-inch pie shell:

1 cup all-purpose flour
4 tablespoons butter or margarine, softened
¼ cup packed light brown sugar
1 square (1 ounce) unsweetened chocolate, grated
1 teaspoon vanilla
2 teaspoons milk
¾ cup finely chopped walnuts

Preheat oven to 375°F.

In a medium-size bowl, mix flour, butter, sugar, and chocolate, using a pastry blender, until mixture resembles coarse crumbs. Add vanilla, milk, and walnuts and mix well. The mixture should be moist enough to form a soft but not sticky dough. If it is too dry, add more milk, a few drops at a time. If sticky, chill until firm.

Press in bottom and up sides of a 9-inch pie plate. Crimp edges with the tines of a fork dipped in flour. Prick all over bottom and sides with the fork. Press a 12-inch square of heavy-duty foil snugly against bottom and sides of shell. Bake for 8 minutes. Remove foil and bake about 10 minutes longer, until crust is dry and crisp. Cool on rack.

Durand R. Cook
Anchorage, Alaska
Anchorage Fur
Rendezvous

Graham Cracker Crust I

For 1 9-inch pie shell:

1½ cups graham cracker crumbs
5⅓ tablespoons butter, melted
3 tablespoons sugar

Preheat oven to 350°F.
Mix everything together and press into pie pan.
Bake for 10 minutes. Cool before filling.

Lois Auernheimer
Fresno, California
Fresno Fair

Graham Cracker Crust II

For 1 9-inch pie shell: 1⅔ cups graham cracker crumbs
¼ cup sugar
5⅓ tablespoons margarine, melted

Blend crumbs with sugar and margarine. Press into a 9-inch pie plate and chill for 30 minutes.

Mrs. Geraldean Roy
Ft. Pierce, Florida
St. Lucie County Fair

Chocolate Graham Cracker Crust

A delicious variation on an old favorite.

For 1 9-inch 1½ cups graham cracker crumbs
pie shell: ¼ cup brown sugar
⅛ teaspoon nutmeg
5⅓ tablespoons butter or margarine, melted
1 square (1 ounce) unsweetened chocolate, melted

Blend graham cracker crumbs with sugar, nutmeg, butter, and chocolate. Press into a 9-inch pie pan. Chill until firm.

Lorna Reed
Anchorage, Alaska
Anchorage Fur
Rendezvous

THE PIES

 # Alaskan Snow Pie

1 Chocolate Graham Cracker Crust (page 26)

Filling,
First Layer:
4 ounces cream cheese, softened
½ cup confectioners' sugar
½ cup heavy cream, whipped

Blend cream cheese and sugar together, then fold in whipped cream. Spread evenly on bottom of chilled pie shell.

Second Layer:
3 ounces chocolate chips
4 ounces cream cheese
¼ cup plus 2 tablespoons light brown sugar
1 teaspoon vanilla extract
1 egg, separated
Dash of salt
½ cup heavy cream, whipped
½ teaspoon nutmeg

Melt chocolate chips over hot water and set aside to cool for 10 minutes. Blend cream cheese, ¼ cup brown sugar, and vanilla. Beat in egg yolk and chocolate.

Beat egg white until stiff (but not dry) and gradually beat in 2 tablespoons brown sugar and dash of salt. Fold into chocolate mixture. Fold in whipped cream. Spread evenly over first layer of pie. Sprinkle with nutmeg. Cool overnight to set.

Lorna Reed
Anchorage, Alaska
Anchorage Fur
Rendezvous

Almond Pie

1 unbaked 9-inch pie shell

Filling: ¼ pound butter, melted
1 cup sugar
3 eggs, beaten
¾ cup light corn syrup
¼ teaspoon salt
1 teaspoon vanilla extract
2 cups chopped almonds

Preheat oven to 375°F.

Combine butter, sugar, eggs, corn syrup, salt, and vanilla in a bowl. Beat until well mixed. Fold in almonds and turn into unbaked pie shell. Bake for 40 to 50 minutes. Cool on rack.

Rita Dolio
Madera, California
Madera
District Fair

California Almond Pie

1 unbaked 9-inch pie shell

Filling: ½ cup light brown sugar
2 tablespoons cake flour
1¼ cups light corn syrup
3 tablespoons butter
¼ teaspoon salt
3 eggs
1 teaspoon vanilla extract
½ teaspoon almond extract
1½ cups sliced almonds

Preheat oven to 350°F.

Mix brown sugar and flour in a saucepan. Add corn syrup, butter, and salt, and warm over low heat just until butter melts. Beat eggs with vanilla and almond extracts. Add to sugar mixture and stir. Turn into unbaked 9-inch pie shell. Sprinkle with almonds. Bake for 35 to 40 minutes.

Diane Kirk
Madera, California
Madera
District Fair

 # Angel Pie

This pie has a meringue crust and a lemon filling.

Meringue Crust:
4 egg whites
¼ teaspoon cream of tartar
1 cup sugar

Preheat oven to 275°F.
Beat egg whites until firm. Add cream of tartar and continue beating. Gradually add the sugar and beat until egg whites are stiff.
Grease a deep, 10-inch pie pan with butter. Pour in meringue mixture and spread to edges. Bake 20 minutes at 275°F, then raise oven heat to 300°F and bake 40 minutes longer. Remove and let cool.

Filling:
4 egg yolks
Grated rind of 1 large lemon
3 tablespoons lemon juice
3 tablespoons hot water
½ cup sugar
½ pint heavy cream (or 1 large container Cool Whip or other whipped topping)

Combine egg yolks, lemon rind, lemon juice, water, and sugar in the top of a double boiler. Cook over simmering water, stirring frequently, until thick. Let cool.
Whip cream until stiff and combine all but one-quarter of it with lemon filling. Mix well. Pour into meringue crust, spreading evenly. Cover with remaining whipped cream. Refrigerate for several hours before serving. The meringue shrinks and cracks while cooling, but the pie keeps well.

Isabel Hazen
Livermore,
California
Alameda
County Fair

Note: Recipe may be halved for a smaller pie or increased by half again (6 eggs) for two 8-inch pies. The meringue crust is also good with a chocolate filling.

Katie's Apple Pie

Katie Gilbert has won more than six hundred prizes in baking and canning since 1941 when she began to enter cooking contests. Katie's Apple Pie won Grand Champion at the Dixie Classic Fair.

1 unbaked 9-inch pie shell
(Boiling Water Pastry, page 18)

Filling: ½ cup sugar
2 tablespoons flour
Pinch of salt
¼ teaspoon cinnamon
½ teaspoon allspice
4 to 5 apples, peeled and sliced
(Mrs. Gilbert prefers Stayman apples)
1 tablespoon lemon juice
2 tablespoons butter, melted (more if you prefer)

Preheat oven to 425°F.
Combine dry ingredients, then stir into apples. Add lemon juice and melted butter and stir well. Turn apples into unbaked pie shell. Cover with topping.

Topping: ½ cup flour
½ cup light brown sugar
4 to 5 tablespoons butter

Mix together until crumbly. Sprinkle over apples. Bake at 425°F for 10 minutes, then reduce oven heat to 350°F and bake for 40 to 45 minutes longer, or until top is browned.

Mrs. Katie Gilbert
Germanton,
North Carolina
Dixie Classic Fair

Linda's Apple Pie

2 unbaked 9-inch pie shells with top crusts
(Oil Pie Crust, page 17)

Filling: 6 large McIntosh apples
(a few more if they are small)
2 cups sugar
2 teaspoons cinnamon
3 tablespoons quick-cooking tapioca
¼ pound butter or margarine

Preheat oven to 425°F.

Peel and slice apples into a bowl of salted water. Drain, leaving just a little of the water for juice. Add sugar, cinnamon, and tapioca. Mix well. Spoon apples into 2 unbaked pie shells, and dot each one with 5 slices of butter or margarine. Cover with top crusts, flute edges, and vent tops. Bake at 425°F for 15 minutes, then reduce oven heat to 350°F and continue baking for 45 minutes.

Linda Hebert
Louisville, Kentucky
Southeast
Washington
State Fair
Walla Walla,
Washington

Delicious Apple Pie

Joyce Zerbe calls her recipe "Delicious Apple Pie," describing the taste, not the variety of apples. She entered a cooking contest for the first time last year and walked off with three first prizes.

1 unbaked 9-inch pie shell with top crust

Filling: **¾ cup sugar**
¼ cup flour
¼ teaspoon nutmeg
¼ teaspoon cinnamon
6 cups thinly sliced tart apples (6 medium apples)
2 tablespoons butter or margarine
¼ cup milk (to brush top of pie)

Preheat oven to 425°F.

Sift sugar, flour, nutmeg, and cinnamon together. Mix with apples. Turn into unbaked pie shell. Dot with butter or margarine. Cover with top crust, flute edges, and vent top. Brush top crust with milk for a golden color. Bake for 40 to 50 minutes, until juice bubbles through slits.

Joyce Zerbe
Bernville,
Pennsylvania
Reading Fair

Apple Custard Pie

1 unbaked 9-inch pie shell
(Never-Fail Pie Crust, page 16)

Filling: 6 cups peeled and sliced tart apples
¾ cup sugar
3 tablespoons flour
½ teaspoon salt
¼ cup light cream or half-and-half
¼ teaspoon cinnamon

Preheat oven to 350°F.

Arrange apples in unbaked pie shell. Combine sugar, flour, salt, and cream, and mix well. Pour over apples. Sprinkle with cinnamon. Cover with a square of aluminum foil. Bake 1 hour. Remove foil and bake 15 minutes longer, or until apples are done.

Note: If you prefer a juicier pie, increase cream by 2 to 3 tablespoons. This will also make it more custardy.

Bonnie Read
Naples, Florida
Collier County Fair

 # Apple-Pecan Pie

Mrs. Woods urged me to try her blue-ribbon recipe for Apple-Pecan Pie whether it was included in the book or not. I did, and now I urge everyone else to try it, too.

1 unbaked 9-inch pie shell

Filling: **6 cups peeled and sliced apples**
½ cup light brown sugar
¼ cup granulated sugar
½ teaspoon salt
2 tablespoons flour
¼ teaspoon nutmeg
½ teaspoon cinnamon
1 tablespoon lemon juice
1 tablespoon butter

Topping: **¼ cup light brown sugar**
¼ cup flour
2 tablespoons butter
½ cup chopped pecans

Preheat oven to 425°F.

Steam the apple slices in 1 or 2 tablespoons water in a covered saucepan for 5 minutes. Remove from heat and add the sugars, salt, flour, nutmeg, cinnamon, lemon juice, and butter. Mix well and turn into unbaked pie shell.

Prepare topping: Blend sugar, flour, and butter. Sprinkle on top of pie. Sprinkle nuts over pie topping.

Cover top of pie with foil and bake at 425°F for 15 minutes, then reduce oven heat to 375°F, remove foil, and bake for 30 to 40 minutes longer.

*Mrs. William
A. Woods
Spring Hill, Florida
Lawrence
County Fair
Bedford, Illinois*

 # Apricot Pie

1 baked 9-inch pie shell

Filling: 2 cups diced dried apricots
1½ cups water
1¼ cups sugar
3 tablespoons flour
½ teaspoon salt
3 egg yolks, beaten
2 tablespoons butter
2 bananas

Meringue: 3 egg whites
¼ teaspoon cream of tartar
6 tablespoons sugar
½ teaspoon vanilla extract

Combine apricots and water in a saucepan. Bring to a boil, reduce heat, cover, and simmer 10 minutes, or until tender. Combine the sugar, flour, and salt; stir into apricots. Bring to a boil and cook 2 minutes, stirring constantly, or use a double boiler. Stir some of the hot mixture into the beaten egg yolks, then return warmed egg yolks to hot mixture and cook for a few minutes until thickened. Remove from heat, stir in butter, and allow to cool.

Preheat oven to 350°F.

Slice bananas and arrange in bottom of pie shell. Top with apricot mixture.

Prepare meringue: Whip egg whites until frothy. Beat in cream of tartar and continue beating until peaks start to form. Beat in sugar, 1 tablespoon at a time, then beat in vanilla. Spread meringue over filling, sealing to edge of pastry. Bake for 12 to 15 minutes, until meringue is golden brown.

Dorothy Watts
Rantoul, Illinois
Champaign County Fair

Autumn Glory Pie

The orange-flavored pie crust and silky apricot filling make this pie a year-round favorite.

1 unbaked 9-inch pie shell, with pastry for lattice top (Orange-Flavored Pastry, page 21)

Filling: **1 can (30 ounces) apricot halves, drained, reserving 1⅔ cups liquid**
½ cup sugar
2 tablespoons cornstarch
Dash of salt
1 cup raisins
1½ teaspoons grated lemon rind
2 tablespoons butter or margarine

Preheat oven to 400°F.

In a large saucepan, combine apricot liquid, sugar, cornstarch, and salt. Cook over medium heat until mixture boils and thickens, stirring constantly. Remove from heat. Stir in apricots, raisins, lemon peel, and butter or margarine. Pour filling into pie shell.

Roll out remaining dough to ⅛-inch thickness: cut into ½-inch strips. Arrange pastry strips in lattice pattern and flute edges. Bake for 20 to 25 minutes, or until crust is golden brown and filling is bubbly.

Ron Stanford
South Gate,
California
L.A. County Fair

Avocado Pie

1 8- or 9-inch graham cracker crust

Filling: 1 large avocado
¼ cup lemon juice
2 egg yolks
1 teaspoon vanilla extract
1 can (14 ounces) Eagle Brand sweetened
condensed milk
½ teaspoon salt

Preheat oven to 325°F.
Cut avocado in half and remove the pit. Peel the avocado halves and cut into ½-inch slices. Mix with lemon juice. Beat egg yolks until thick; add avocado and vanilla. Continue beating; add condensed milk and salt. Beat until smooth. Pour into graham cracker crust. Bake for 20 minutes. Let cool. Prepare topping.

Topping: ½ pint sour cream
¼ cup sugar
½ teaspoon vanilla extract

Beat ingredients together. Pour over pie and chill thoroughly before serving.

Susan Westover
Dallas, Texas
State Fair of Texas

Banana Cream Pie

1 baked 9-inch pie shell

Filling: ⅔ cup sugar
3 tablespoons cornstarch
¼ teaspoon salt
3 egg yolks
1 cup evaporated milk
1 cup water
1 teaspoon vanilla extract
1½ cups sliced bananas
Whipped cream or whipped topping

Mix sugar, cornstarch, salt, and egg yolks together thoroughly in a saucepan. Combine evaporated milk and water; stir into sugar mixture until smooth. Cook over low heat, stirring until thickened, about 10 minutes. Remove from heat, stir in vanilla, and let cool completely.

Arrange bananas in baked pie shell. Cover with cool custard. Spread with whipped cream or whipped topping and refrigerate.

Mary Davies
Oklahoma City,
Oklahoma
Oklahoma
State Fair

Fresh Blackberry Pie

1 unbaked 9-inch pie shell with top crust

Filling:
1 cup sugar
5 tablespoons flour
½ teaspoon cinnamon
¼ teaspoon salt
4 cups fresh blackberries
2 tablespoons butter

Preheat oven to 425°F.

Mix sugar, flour, cinnamon, and salt together and carefully blend through the berries. Pour berries into unbaked pie shell. Dot with butter. Cover with top crust, flute edges, and vent top. Bake at 425°F for 15 minutes, then reduce oven heat to 350°F and bake for 30 minutes longer, or until golden brown.

Curt Webber
Fresno, California
Fresno Fair

 # Blackberry Jam Pie

This pie has been made by Mrs. Parsons' family for more than sixty-five years. Mrs. Parsons, who has been cooking since she was fourteen, is now in her seventies.

1 baked 9-inch pie shell

Filling: **3 egg yolks**
¾ cup sugar
1 teaspoon vanilla extract
1 cup blackberry jam
2 tablespoons flour
1 cup buttermilk

Meringue: **2 egg whites**
¼ teaspoon cream of tartar
4 tablespoons confectioners' sugar
½ teaspoon vanilla extract

Preheat oven to 350°F.

Combine all the filling ingredients in the top of a double boiler. Cook, stirring, over hot water until mixture thickens to custard consistency. Remove from heat and beat with a wooden spoon until slightly cooled.

Prepare meringue. Whip egg whites until frothy. Beat in cream of tartar and continue beating until peaks start to form. Beat in confectioners' sugar, 1 tablespoon at a time, then beat in vanilla.

Pour custard filling into baked pie shell. Cover with meringue. Bake for 10 to 15 minutes.

Mrs. H.V. Parsons
West Monroe,
Louisiana
Louisiana State Fair

 # Black Bottom Pie

1 baked 8-inch pie shell

Filling: ½ cup plus ⅓ cup sugar
2 tablespoons cornstarch
½ teaspoon salt
2 eggs, separated
2 cups milk
2 teaspoons unflavored gelatin
3 tablespoons cold water
2 tablespoons rum
1 square (1 ounce) unsweetened chocolate,
   melted and cooled
¼ teaspoon cream of tartar

Blend ½ cup sugar, cornstarch, and salt together in a saucepan. Lightly beat egg yolks with a fork and stir in milk. Add milk mixture to dry ingredients in saucepan; cook over medium heat, stirring constantly, until mixture just comes to a boil. Remove from heat. Reserve 1 cup of this mixture and set aside.

Dissolve gelatin in cold water and stir into remaining milk mixture. Stir in rum. Place in refrigerator and chill, stirring occasionally, until mixture mounds slightly when dropped from a spoon.

Combine melted chocolate with reserved 1 cup of filling and pour in the bottom of baked pie shell.

Beat egg whites and cream of tartar until foamy. Slowly beat in ⅓ cup sugar until mixture is stiff and glossy. Fold in rum custard mixture, then spread on top of chocolate layer in crust. Chill 2 to 3 hours before serving. Garnish with whipped cream, if desired.

Nikki Niccum
Anaheim, California
L.A. County Fair

44

Old-Fashioned Blueberry Pie

1 unbaked 10-inch pie shell with top crust
(Margarine Pastry, page 13)

Filling: 3 cups fresh or frozen (unthawed) blueberries
1¼ cups plus 1 tablespoon sugar
1 tablespoon lemon juice
3 tablespoons quick-cooking tapioca
½ teaspoon cinnamon
1 tablespoon butter or margarine

Preheat oven to 400°F.

In a bowl, mix together blueberries, 1¼ cups sugar, lemon juice, and tapioca. Pour into unbaked pie shell. Sprinkle with cinnamon and dot with butter or margarine. Cover with top crust, flute edges, and vent top. Sprinkle top crust with 1 tablespoon sugar and bake for 40 to 50 minutes. If crust starts to darken before the pie is done, cut foil strips to lay over the edges.

Mrs. Colleen K.
Teichman
Kalispell, Montana
Northwest
Montana Fair

 # Blueberry-Peach Pie

The pie shell and lattice top are baked on their own, the filling precooked, and the whole assembled into a delicious and unusual pie. This pie won a first place in the Peach Pie Division of the Fresno Fair.

**1 baked 9-inch pie shell and lattice top
(Crisco Pie Crust, page 15)**

Filling: **2 cans (29 ounces each) sliced peaches
(or 4 cups fresh sliced peaches)
½ cup sugar
1 envelope unflavored gelatin
2 tablespoons cornstarch
⅓ cup orange juice
3 tablespoons brandy
2 tablespoons lemon juice
1 tablespoon butter
1 cup fresh or frozen and thawed blueberries**

Drain peaches well, reserving 1¼ cups syrup. Reserve a few peach slices for garnish. In a saucepan, combine sugar, gelatin, cornstarch, orange juice, and reserved peach syrup. Cook, stirring, until thick and clear. Stir in brandy, lemon juice, and butter. Fold in peaches, then drained blueberries. Turn mixture into baked pie shell. Top with pastry strips. Chill until firm. Garnish with reserved peaches.

Note: If using fresh or home-canned peaches, add apple juice or orange juice to make 1¼ cups syrup. Increase sugar to ¾ cup for fresh peaches.

*Arleen Owen
Fresno, California
Fresno Fair*

Blueberry Pie Supreme

1 9-inch graham cracker pie crust

Filling: 1 can (1 pound, 5 ounces) blueberry pie filling
12 ounces softened cream cheese
(four 3-ounce packages)
½ cup sugar
2 eggs
½ teaspoon vanilla extract
1 cup sour cream

Preheat oven to 425°F.

Spread half of blueberry pie filling over bottom of pie crust; reserve the rest. Heat pie crust in oven for 5 minutes and remove. Reduce oven temperature to 350°F.

While pie crust is in oven, beat cream cheese with sugar, eggs, and vanilla until smooth. Pour into warmed pie crust (over blueberry filling). Bake 25 minutes at 350°F. Filling will be slightly soft in center. Cool completely on wire rack. Spoon sour cream around edge of pie and fill center with remaining blueberry pie filling.

Note: If you buy two 8-ounce packages of cream cheese and use 12 ounces in the recipe, the remaining 4 ounces can be whipped into the sour cream to stiffen it and make it stand up a little better.

Linda M. Shifflet
Anaheim, California
Orange County Fair

Boysenberry Custard Pie

1 baked 9-inch pie shell

Filling: 1½ cups milk
1½ cups sugar
⅛ teaspoon salt
3 teaspoons plus 2 tablespoons cornstarch
3 egg yolks
½ cup sour cream
1 teaspoon vanilla extract
2⅓ cups boysenberries
2 tablespoons cornstarch
1 tablespoon lime juice
1 tablespoon butter

Heat milk in a saucepan. Stir ¾ cup sugar, salt, and 3 teaspoons cornstarch into milk and cook, stirring frequently, until thickened. Beat egg yolks in a small bowl. Beat ¼ cup of hot mixture into egg yolks a little at a time. When egg yolks are warmed, pour them slowly into hot mixture, stirring continuously. Cook, stirring frequently, for 12 minutes. Remove from heat. Add sour cream and vanilla and mix well. Let cool.

Heat boysenberries in a saucepan. Stir in ¾ cup sugar and 2 tablespoons cornstarch. Cook for 4 minutes. Remove from heat. Stir in lime juice and butter. Let cool.

Pour cooled custard into baked pie shell. Top with boysenberries. Chill before serving. Garnish with whipped cream, if desired.

Tommie Arenas
Fresno, California
Fresno Fair

Brandy Alexander Pie

1 baked 8-inch pie shell

Filling: 3 cups mini-marshmallows
½ cup milk
1 chocolate bar with almonds (8 ounces)
¼ cup dark creme de cacao
3 tablespoons cognac
2 cups heavy cream

In a saucepan, heat marshmallows and milk over low heat just until marshmallows melt. Add three-quarters of the chocolate bar to the melting marshmallows and reserve the rest. Stir to blend, then chill mixture until slightly thickened. Blend in creme de cacao and cognac.

In a chilled bowl, beat the cream until stiff. Fold marshmallow mixture into whipped cream. Pour into baked pie crust. Shred or grate remaining chocolate bar and sprinkle over pie to garnish. Chill completely before serving.

Zoe TeBeau
Edmond, Oklahoma
Oklahoma
State Fair

Buttermilk Raisin Pie

1 baked 9-inch pie shell

Filling: 6 tablespoons flour
¾ cup sugar
¼ teaspoon salt
2 cups buttermilk
1¼ cups seedless raisins
3 egg yolks
2 tablespoons lemon juice
2 tablespoons butter
⅓ teaspoon cinnamon
⅛ teaspoon cloves
¼ teaspoon nutmeg

Meringue: 3 egg whites
2 tablespoons sugar
¼ teaspoon cinnamon
⅛ teaspoon nutmeg

Preheat oven to 350°F.

Combine the flour, sugar, and salt in a saucepan. Gradually stir in the buttermilk. Cook, stirring, over low heat until the mixture is thick. Add the raisins and turn heat very low. Beat the egg yolks in a bowl and gradually stir in some of the hot mixture. When egg yolks are warmed, stir them gradually into the hot mixture. Cook, stirring constantly, for 1 to 2 minutes longer. Remove from heat and cool several minutes. Stir in lemon juice, butter, and spices. Cool to room temperature, then turn into baked pie shell.

Prepare meringue: Beat egg whites until they form soft peaks. Add sugar and spices a little at a time, beating until egg whites form stiff peaks. Spread meringue over the pie. Bake for 15 to 20 minutes, or until golden brown.

Gwen Deniz
Madera, California
Madera
District Fair

 # Butterscotch Pie

"This recipe was used by my mother when she was in high school home-economics class," writes Carol Sisler. More recently it has won prizes at the Ionia County Free Fair. It is very rich and very good.

1 baked 9-inch pie shell (Basic Pie Crust, page 11)

Filling: 1½ cups light brown sugar
¼ teaspoon salt
2 tablespoons flour
3 tablespoons cornstarch
1½ cups hot water
2 egg yolks
1 tablespoon butter
1 teaspoon vanilla extract

Mix together sugar, salt, flour, and cornstarch in a saucepan. Add hot water, stirring well. Cook until thick and clear. Beat egg yolks. Add a small amount of hot mixture to egg yolks and mix well. Slowly pour egg yolks into hot sugar mixture, stirring constantly. Cook, stirring, over low heat for 1 minute. Remove from heat and stir in butter and vanilla. Cool slightly, then pour into baked pie shell. Prepare the meringue.

Meringue: 2 egg whites
¼ teaspoon cream of tartar
½ teaspoon vanilla extract
4 tablespoons sugar

Preheat oven to 350°F.
Beat egg whites with cream of tartar and vanilla until soft peaks start to form. Gradually add the sugar, beating until stiff peaks form and all the sugar is dissolved. Spread meringue mixture on top of pie, making a seal with the pastry edges. Bake for 12 to 15 minutes, or until meringue is golden. Let cool before serving.

Carol Sisler
Orleans, Michigan
Ionia County
Free Fair

Creamed Cheese Cake

Anita Wisniewski's family recipe for cheesecake has won first prize at the New Hampshire State Fair, the Sandwich Fair, and the Fryeburg Fair in Maine. It is baked in a springform pan, which makes it easy to remove before serving.

16 ounces cream cheese, softened
16 ounces creamed cottage cheese
1½ cups sugar
4 eggs, lightly beaten
2 tablespoons lemon juice
1 teaspoon vanilla extract
3 tablespoons flour
3 tablespoons cornstarch
½ pound butter, softened
16 ounces sour cream

Preheat oven to 325°F.

Beat cream cheese together with cottage cheese to blend. Gradually beat in sugar, then eggs, beating until smooth. Stir in lemon juice, vanilla, flour, and cornstarch. Beat in butter until smooth, then blend in sour cream. Pour into greased 9-inch springform pan. Bake for 1 hour. Turn off oven and leave cheesecake for 2 hours inside oven. *Do not open oven at any time.*

Chill in refrigerator before serving.

Anita Wisniewski
Danbury,
New Hampshire
New Hampshire
State Fair

Blueberry Cheesecake

Mrs. Distifeno uses fresh blueberries for her blue-ribbon cheesecake when they are in season, but says that frozen blueberries work just as well. The cheesecake is gorgeous, and just as delicious as it looks.

2 pounds cream cheese, softened
6 eggs
1½ cups sugar
3 tablespoons cornstarch
3 tablespoons flour
1½ tablespoons vanilla extract
1 tablespoon lemon juice
½ cup sour cream
1 cup heavy cream
¼ pound butter, melted
1¾ cups fresh or frozen blueberries
1 can (21 ounces) blueberry pie filling

Preheat oven to 350°F.

In a bowl, combine cream cheese, eggs, sugar, cornstarch, flour, vanilla, and lemon juice. Blend in sour cream, heavy cream, butter, and blueberries. Pour into buttered 9-inch springform pan and bake for 1 hour. Turn oven off, and cool 1 hour in oven. Remove to rack to cool completely.

Preheat oven to 400°F.

Spread blueberry pie filling evenly over top of cooled cheesecake. Bake for 15 minutes. Cool and refrigerate for several hours before serving.

Phyllis L. Distifeno
Beaverton, Oregon
Oregon State Fair

 # Dairyman's Delight

This delicious cheesecake pie won a refrigerator-freezer for Esther Mishler.

2 cups graham cracker crumbs
¼ pound butter, melted
½ cup lemon juice
1 cup heavy cream
1 package (8 ounces) cream cheese
1 can sweetened condensed milk
¼ cup cold water
1 envelope plain gelatin
1 teaspoon vanilla extract
1 cup sour cream

Mix graham cracker crumbs and butter together. Press three-quarters of mixture into a 9-inch pie plate.

Stir lemon juice into cream and let stand 10 minutes. In a mixing bowl, mash cream cheese with a fork. Gradually beat in condensed milk and mix until smooth.

Place the cold water in the top of a double boiler and sprinkle gelatin over it. Let gelatin dissolve over boiling water.

Whip lemon-cream mixture until it begins to stiffen. Pour in cream cheese mixture and continue beating until well blended. Stir in gelatin and vanilla. Pour into crumb-lined pan and sprinkle top with remains of cracker crumbs. Spread top with sour cream. Refrigerate for at least 2 hours before serving.

Esther Mishler
Hollsopple,
Pennsylvania
Pennsylvania
State Farm Show

Cherry Pie

1 unbaked 9-inch pie shell with top crust

Filling: **4 tablespoons quick-cooking tapioca**
⅛ teaspoon salt
1 cup sugar
4 cups pitted cherries
¼ teaspoon almond extract
1 tablespoon butter

Preheat oven to 400°F.

Combine tapioca, salt, sugar, cherries, and almond extract, and let stand 15 minutes. Turn into unbaked pie shell and dot with butter. Cover with top crust, flute edges, and vent top. Bake for 50 minutes.

Note: It's best to put pie on a cookie sheet while it's baking because it runs over.

Shirley A. Schultz
Horicon, Wisconsin
Dodge County Fair

Luke's Cherry Pie

1 baked 9-inch pie shell

Filling: 1 envelope unflavored gelatin
2 tablespoons cold water
1 quart cherries, pitted
1 cup sugar
2 tablespoons cornstarch
4 teaspoons lemon juice

Soak gelatin in cold water and set aside. Mash half of the cherries with sugar. Stir in cornstarch and lemon juice. Cook over medium heat until thick and transparent. Remove from heat. Add gelatin and stir briskly.

Slice remaining cherries into baked pie shell. Pour gelatin mixture over the sliced cherries. Refrigerate for several hours before serving.

J. Luke Sluski
Lakeland, Florida
Florida State Fair

Sour Cherry Pie

2 unbaked 9-inch pie shells with pastry for
  top crusts

Filling: 1½ cups sugar
3 tablespoons cornstarch
Pinch of salt
3 drops almond extract
4 cups pitted sour cherries (frozen or fresh)
Butter or margarine

Preheat oven to 425°F.

Combine sugar, cornstarch, and salt. Add almond
extract and cherries. Mix thoroughly. Pour equal
amounts into unbaked pie shells. Dot with butter
or margarine and cover with top crust. Bake for 40
minutes, or until golden brown.

Joyce Mitchell
Columbus, Ohio
Ohio State Fair

Chess Pie I

1 unbaked 9-inch pie shell

Filling: 1½ cups sugar
¼ pound butter
1 tablespoon water
1 tablespoon vinegar
3 eggs, beaten
1 teaspoon vanilla extract

Preheat oven to 350°F.

Mix sugar, butter, water, and vinegar together in a saucepan. Bring to a boil. Let cool, then blend in the eggs and vanilla. Pour into pie shell and bake for 1 hour.

Kristie Lynn
McKinley
Hendersonville,
Tennessee

Chess Pie II

1 baked 9-inch pie shell

Filling: 1 cup raisins
1 cup water
1 tablespoon butter
1 cup sugar
2 tablespoons flour
1 cup milk
3 egg yolks
1 cup chopped peanuts
1 teaspoon vanilla extract

Boil raisins in water for about 30 minutes, or until tender. Add the butter and sugar. Dissolve the flour in a little bit of the milk and add it with remaining milk. Cook, stirring frequently, until thickened. Beat egg yolks. Add a little of the hot mixture to the yolks, mix well, and when egg yolks are warmed, stir into hot mixture. Cook 2 to 3 minutes longer and remove from heat. Add peanuts and vanilla. Let cool to room temperature. Stir and pour into baked pie shell. Top with whipped cream, if desired.

Sandra Bewick
Anchorage, Alaska
Anchorage Fur
Rendezvous

 # Chess Tarts

Mrs. Shouse writes that this recipe came from her husband's aunt many years ago and "it has never failed me. It is always requested at family gatherings. And has won many prizes." The individual tarts have great charm, and their delicious taste makes them justifiably popular.

12 unbaked, individual 3-inch tart shells (Mrs. Shouse makes them in aluminum foil tins), using Basic Pie Crust (page 11)

Filling: **1½ cups light brown sugar**
1 tablespoon flour
4 tablespoons butter or margarine, softened
2 eggs
2 tablespoons water
1 teaspoon vanilla extract

Preheat oven to 375°F.

Mix sugar with flour and beat into butter or margarine until a creamy consistency. Beat eggs with water, then combine with sugar-butter mixture. Mix well, then add vanilla. Beat continuously until mixture is light and fluffy.

Fill tart shells two-thirds full with filling mixture. Bake for about 30 minutes, or until firm. Let cool before serving.

Note: This filling recipe is excellent for pecan pie. Pour filling into unbaked 8- or 9-inch pie shell. Top with 1 cup pecans. Bake as above.

Mrs. La Rue H.
Shouse
Winston-Salem,
North Carolina
Dixie Classic Fair

Chocolate Pie

This family recipe took first prize at the Lincoln County Fair in Tennessee.

1 baked 9-inch pie shell

Filling: **¼ cup cocoa**
1½ cups sugar
5 tablespoons flour
½ teaspoon salt
3 egg yolks, beaten
2 cups milk
2 teaspoons vanilla extract
2 tablespoons butter

Combine cocoa, sugar, flour, and salt together in a heavy saucepan. Add egg yolks, milk, and vanilla. Cook over low heat, stirring frequently, for 10 minutes, or until mixture thickens. Remove from heat and stir in butter. Let cool a little before pouring into baked pie shell.

If you wish, top with meringue or whipped cream.

*Sheila Womack
Fayetteville,
Tennessee
Lincoln County Fair*

Chocolate Cream Pie

1 baked 9-inch pie shell

Filling 1: 6 ounces cream cheese
¾ cup confectioners' sugar
¾ cup heavy cream, whipped and sweetened
to taste

Blend cream cheese and sugar till smooth. Fold in whipped cream. Spread over cooled crust. Refrigerate.

Filling 2: ¾ cup sugar
4 tablespoons cornstarch
6 tablespoons cocoa (Hershey's preferred)
2 cups milk
3 egg yolks, beaten
2 tablespoons butter
1 teaspoon vanilla extract
1 cup heavy cream, whipped
Mini chocolate chips or chocolate leaves

Combine sugar, cornstarch, and cocoa. Gradually add milk to egg yolks. Slowly add milk mixture to dry ingredients, stirring to prevent lumps. Cook over medium heat, stirring constantly, till it boils. Boil 2 minutes. Remove from heat; stir in butter and vanilla. Cool completely. Pour into shell over cream cheese layer. Garnish with whipped cream and decorate with chocolate chips or chocolate leaves.

Joy McAlister
Ontario, California
L.A. County Fair

 # Coconut Cream Pie

Mrs. Adenau raised a large family, so she has had a lot of practice cooking. She bakes weekly for her church bingo fund-raising social, and enters her baked goods in county fairs. Her coconut cream pie won a first at the Oregon State Fair.

1 baked 9-inch pie shell

Filling: ⅔ **cup sugar**
¼ cup cornstarch
½ teaspoon salt
3 cups milk
4 egg yolks, slightly beaten
2 tablespoons margarine
2 teaspoons vanilla extract
¾ cup flaked coconut
1 cup heavy cream, chilled
1 teaspoon confectioners' sugar
¼ cup toasted coconut

Mix sugar, cornstarch, and salt together in a saucepan. Blend milk and egg yolks, then gradually stir into sugar mixture. Cook over medium heat, stirring constantly, until mixture thickens and boils. Boil, stirring constantly, for 1 minute, and remove from heat. Stir in margarine, vanilla, and flaked coconut. Let cool. Pour into baked pie shell and cover with plastic wrap. Chill pie thoroughly at least 2 hours.

Whip cream together with confectioners' sugar until stiff. Spread evenly over pie and sprinkle with toasted coconut.

Note: The filling may be cooked entirely in a microwave oven. Combine all ingredients and cook for 7 minutes on high.

Jean Ann Adenau
St. Helens, Oregon
Oregon State Fair

Coconut-Pinto Bean Pie

Here is a pie that proudly proclaims its American Southwest heritage.

1 unbaked 9-inch pie shell

Filling: **1 cup cooked pinto beans**
1 cup sugar
1 cup dark corn syrup
4 eggs
½ cup shredded coconut

Preheat oven to 400°F.

Mash pinto beans. Add sugar, syrup, and unbeaten eggs. Beat together with a wooden spoon until sugar is dissolved. Stir in coconut. Pour into unbaked pie shell. Bake for 10 minutes at 400°F, then turn down oven heat to 375°F and bake another 20 minutes. Let cool before serving.

Robert Sowards
Casa Grande,
Arizona
Pinal County Fair

Blum's Coffee Toffee Pie

1 baked Nutty Chocolate Pie Dough (page 23)

Filling: ¼ pound butter, softened
¾ cup sugar
2 teaspoons instant coffee powder
1 square (1 ounce) unsweetened chocolate, melted
2 eggs

With electric mixer, beat butter in a large bowl until light and fluffy. Gradually add the sugar, beating on high speed. Beat in instant coffee and melted chocolate. Add eggs, one at a time, beating on high speed 5 minutes after each egg. Spread filling evenly in cooled pie shell. Cover and refrigerate at least 6 hours before serving.

Topping: 1½ cups chilled heavy cream
6 tablespoons confectioners' sugar
1½ tablespoons instant coffee powder
Chocolate curls

With electric mixer, beat cream, confectioners' sugar, and instant coffee in a large bowl until stiff peaks form. Drop dollops of cream around edges of pie. Arrange a few chocolate curls in center. Refrigerate at least 2 hours before serving.

Durand R. Cook
Anchorage, Alaska
Anchorage Fur
Rendezvous

Custard Pie

This custard pie never weeps, and it always wins a prize for Emma Williams, who is eighty-four years old.

1 unbaked 9-inch pie shell

Filling: **2¾ cups milk**
4 tablespoons margarine
3 eggs
1 cup sugar
1 teaspoon vanilla extract
1 teaspoon nutmeg

Preheat oven to 450°F.

Scald milk and margarine together. Whip eggs until they turn pale, add sugar, and whip for 10 minutes more. Beat a little of the hot milk into the eggs, and when they are warmed, stir eggs into hot milk. Add vanilla, and sprinkle nutmeg over top.

Prick the bottom of pie crust with the tines of a fork. Bake for 10 minutes at 450°F, then reduce oven heat to 400°F. Pour custard mixture into pie shell and bake at 400°F for 10 minutes, then reduce heat to 350°F and bake 20 minutes longer, or until custard is firm.

Emma Williams
Elizabethtown,
Tennessee

Grape Pie

1 baked 9-inch pie shell

Filling: 8 ounces cream cheese
¾ cup seedless grapes
¾ cup Cool Whip
¾ cup confectioners' sugar

Combine all the ingredients in the bowl of a blender and blend for 30 seconds, or just to mix all ingredients together. Grapes should be chunky; the filling should *not* be liquid. Spread filling in cooled pie shell.

Topping and glaze: 1½ cups seedless grapes (approximately)
1½ ounces lime Jell-O (half a 3-ounce package)
1 teaspoon unflavored gelatin
¾ cup boiling water, plus ½ cup cold water

Arrange grapes on top of pie. Mix Jell-O with unflavored gelatin and dissolve in boiling water. Add the ½ cup cold water and stir. Pour over top of pie, making sure to cover the entire surface. Refrigerate for 4 hours.

Marla Ens
Fresno, California
Fresno Fair

Green Grape-Apple Pie

1 unbaked 9-inch pie shell with top crust

Filling: 2 cups seedless grapes
3 cups sliced apples
1 cup sugar
3 tablespoons quick-cooking tapioca
¼ teaspoon ground cardamom
¼ teaspoon cinnamon
¼ teaspoon salt
2 tablespoons butter

Preheat oven to 425°F.

Combine grapes, apples, sugar, tapioca, spices, and salt. Turn into unbaked pie shell. Dot with butter. Cover with top crust, flute edges, and vent top. Bake for 50 to 60 minutes.

Frances Grajek
Fresno, California
Fresno Fair

Fresh Grapefruit Pie

1 9-inch graham cracker crust
(Graham Cracker Crust II, page 25)

Filling: 1½ cups grapefruit sections
1 cup sugar
1 envelope unflavored gelatin
¼ cup cold water
1 cup heavy cream
2 tablespoons confectioners' sugar
½ teaspoon vanilla extract

Reserve 4 whole grapefruit sections, and cut remaining sections into small pieces. Be careful to save the juice.

Combine fruit, juice, and sugar in a bowl. Let stand 5 minutes. Drain, reserving 1 cup of juice. Bring juice to a simmer. Sprinkle gelatin over cold water to soften, then add to hot juice, and stir until dissolved. Chill in refrigerator until mixture is slightly thicker than consistency of unbeaten egg whites.

Beat cream with confectioners' sugar and vanilla until stiff. Fold whipped cream and fruit into gelatin mixture. Turn into pie shell and decorate with reserved grapefruit sections and a sprinkling of graham cracker crumbs. Chill thoroughly before serving.

Mrs. Geraldean Roy
Ft. Pierce, Florida
St. Lucie County Fair

69

Green Tomato Pie

For three years running, Mrs. Carlson has won the Grand Champion Cook Plaque for Canning and Baking. Baking, she says, is her first love, and this Green Tomato Pie is a good example of her art.

1 unbaked 9-inch pie shell with top crust, or lattice

Filling: **2 cups peeled and sliced green tomatoes**
2 cups plus 1 teaspoon sugar
3 tablespoons flour
½ teaspoon cinnamon
½ teaspoon salt
1½ tablespoons vinegar
1 tablespoon water
1 tablespoon butter

Preheat oven to 425°F.
Place sliced green tomatoes in a bowl. Toss with 2 cups sugar, flour, cinnamon, and salt. Add vinegar and water and mix well. Pour into unbaked pie shell and dot with butter. Cover with top crust or lattice and sprinkle with sugar. Bake at 425°F for 10 minutes, then lower oven heat to 350°F and bake for 30 minutes longer.

Mrs. Faith Carlson
Malden, Illinois
Tri-County Fair

 # Lemon Meringue Pie

Mrs. Leigh writes that her twenty-eight-year-old grandson always says he does not care what she serves for dessert, just so long as it is her lemon pie. Along with accolades from her grandson, her pie has won a blue ribbon as well as Reserve Champion over all.

1 baked 9-inch pie shell

Filling: **1½ cups sugar**
7 tablespoons cornstarch
Dash of salt
1½ cups *hot* water
3 large eggs, separated
1 teaspoon grated lemon rind
2 tablespoons butter or margarine
½ cup lemon juice

In a saucepan, mix the sugar, cornstarch, salt, and hot water and bring to a boil. Cook for 8 minutes, stirring constantly. Beat the egg yolks with a fork, add several tablespoons of hot mixture, then add warmed egg yolks to the sugar mixture and cook 3 minutes more. Remove from heat and stir in grated lemon rind and butter or margarine. Add lemon juice, a little at a time, and mix well. Let cool while preparing meringue.

Meringue: **1 tablespoon cornstarch**
2 tablespoons cold water
½ cup *hot* water
3 egg whites
6 tablespoons sugar
1 teaspoon lemon juice

Preheat oven to 350°F.

Dissolve cornstarch in the cold water. Add to hot water in a small saucepan and boil for 2 minutes. Let cool. Beat the egg whites until stiff and add the sugar 1 tablespoon at a time. Add cornstarch mixture and continue beating. Add lemon juice.

Pour filling into baked 9-inch pie shell and cover with meringue. Make sure to spread meringue to edges of pie. Bake for 15 to 20 minutes, or until golden brown.

Ellen Leigh
Lake Odessa,
Michigan
Ionia County Free Fair

Best-Ever Lemon Pie

"My mother made this pie when I was first learning to bake," writes Ruth Huinker, "and now I have been married for forty-six years and still bake it." And she still wins prizes at the Antelope Valley Fair.

1 baked 9-inch pie shell

Filling: **1¼ cups sugar**
6 tablespoons cornstarch
2 cups water
3 egg yolks
⅓ cup lemon juice
1½ teaspoons lemon extract
3 tablespoons butter
2 teaspoons vinegar

Mix sugar and cornstarch together in top of double boiler. Add the water. Combine egg yolks with lemon juice and beat until foamy. Combine with sugar and cornstarch mixture in top of double boiler. Cook over boiling water until thick, about 25 minutes. Remove from heat and add lemon extract, butter, and vinegar. Stir thoroughly and let cool while preparing meringue.

Never-Fail Meringue: **1 tablespoon cornstarch**
2 tablespoons cold water
½ cup boiling water
3 egg whites
6 tablespoons sugar
1 teaspoon vanilla extract
Pinch of salt

Blend cornstarch and cold water in a saucepan. Add boiling water and cook, stirring, until clear and thickened. Let stand until completely cold. Beat egg whites until foamy. Gradually add sugar and beat until peaks are stiff but not dry. Add vanilla and salt and gradually beat in cornstarch mixture.

Preheat oven to 350°F.

Pour filling into baked pie shell. Spread meringue over filling. Bake for 10 to 15 minutes.

Ruth Huinker
Lancaster,
California
Antelope
Valley Fair

Aunt Dolly's Lemon Sponge Pie

Nancy Lee entered her first competition a year ago with this pie, having decided "to put my money where my mouth is and see if my pies were as good as everyone said." The first prize she received tells the story. The recipe has been handed down from her mother's Aunt Dolly and is at least seventy years old.

1 unbaked 9-inch pie shell

Filling: **¾ cup butter**
1½ cups sugar
5 medium eggs, or 4 large eggs
1½ cups milk
2 heaping tablespoons flour
Juice and grated rind of 2 lemons

Preheat oven to 375°F.
   Cream butter and sugar together. Separate eggs and add egg yolks to butter mixture. Mix well. (Reserve the whites.) Stir milk, flour, lemon juice, and rind into butter mixture. Beat egg whites until stiff and fold gently but thoroughly into butter mixture. Turn into unbaked pie shell. Bake for 1 hour, or until knife inserted in center comes out clean.

Nancy Lee
Fortuna, California
Humboldt
County Fair

Southern Lemon Buttermilk Pie

The recipe for this delicious and unusual pie comes from Mrs. Armstrong's sister-in-law, Mrs. Harry B. Chadwick.

2 unbaked 8-inch pie shells

Filling: **3 large eggs**
¼ pound margarine, at room temperature
2 cups sugar
2 tablespoons flour
2 cups buttermilk
2 teaspoons lemon extract
Pinch of salt

Preheat oven to 350°F.

Beat eggs well. Add margarine and beat well. Mix sugar and flour together and add to the egg mixture. Pour in buttermilk and lemon extract and mix thoroughly. Distribute mixture evenly between two unbaked pie shells. Cut aluminum foil to fit around edge of crust to keep from browning too much. Bake 40 to 45 minutes.

Annie Laurie
Armstrong
Orangeburg,
South Carolina
Orangeburg
County Fair

Lemon Cake Pie

These custardy pies, made from an old family recipe, are so good you might as well make two.

2 unbaked 9-inch pie shells

Filling: **4 egg yolks**
1 cup sugar
2 heaping tablespoons flour
2 cups milk
2 tablespoons butter, melted
½ teaspoon lemon extract
½ teaspoon vanilla extract
4 egg whites, at room temperature

Preheat oven to 350°F.

Beat egg yolks with a fork; add sugar, flour, milk, melted butter, and lemon and vanilla flavorings. Continue beating until well mixed. In a separate bowl, whip egg whites until stiff. Fold egg whites into egg yolk mixture. Pour mixture into unbaked pie shells. Bake 40 minutes, or until firm and brown on top. Cool before serving.

*Mrs. Elizabeth
Anderson
Winston-Salem,
North Carolina
Dixie Classic Fair*

Lemon-Lime
Daiquiri Pie

Coconut 2 cups flaked coconut
Crust: 3 tablespoons butter or margarine

Preheat oven to 325°F.
   Combine coconut and melted butter. Press onto bottom and sides of a 9-inch pie plate. Bake for 20 minutes. Let cool.

Tart Lemon ¾ cup sugar
Filling: 3 tablespoons cornstarch
   ¼ teaspoon salt
   ¾ cup water
   1 teaspoon grated lemon peel
   1 tablespoon butter
   ⅓ cup lemon juice
   4 drops yellow food coloring (optional)

Mix sugar, cornstarch, and salt in a saucepan. Gradually stir in water. Cook, stirring, until mixture thickens and boils. Boil and stir 1 minute. Remove from heat; add lemon peel and butter. Stir in lemon juice and optional food color. Let cool.

Lime Daiquiri 1 cup sugar
Filling: 1 envelope unflavored gelatin
   ¼ teaspoon salt
   ⅓ cup lime juice
   ⅓ cup water
   3 egg yolks, slightly beaten
   ½ teaspoon grated lime peel
   ¼ cup light rum
   3 egg whites

Combine ⅔ cup sugar, gelatin, and salt. Stir in lime juice, water, and egg yolks. Cook and stir over low heat until mixture thickens slightly. Remove from heat; stir in lime peel. Cool slightly; stir in rum. Chill to consistency of corn syrup.

Immediately beat egg whites, gradually adding ⅓ cup sugar until stiff peaks form. Fold egg whites into gelatin mixture. Chill until mixture mounds when dropped from a spoon.

To assemble: Spread cooled lemon filling on baked coconut crust; cover with lime filling. Decorate with whipped cream and chill overnight.

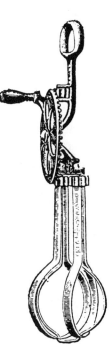

Diane Johnson
McKinney, Texas
State Fair of Texas

Lime Meringue Pie

1 baked 8- or 9-inch pie shell

Filling: 1½ cups sugar
3 tablespoons cornstarch
¼ teaspoon salt
1½ cups *hot* water
3 egg yolks, slightly beaten
2 tablespoons margarine
½ teaspoon grated lime peel
⅓ cup lime juice

Meringue: 3 egg whites
¼ teaspoon cream of tartar
5 tablespoons sugar
½ teaspoon vanilla extract

Preheat oven to 350°F.

In a saucepan, mix sugar, cornstarch, and salt. Gradually add hot water. Cook and stir over high heat until mixture boils. Reduce heat and cook, stirring, 2 minutes longer. Remove from heat.

Stir small amount of hot mixture into egg yolks, then return to hot mix. Bring to a boil and cook 2 minutes, stirring constantly. Add margarine and lime peel. Slowly add lime juice; mix well. Let cool. Pour into baked pie shell.

Prepare meringue: Whip egg whites until frothy. Beat in cream of tartar and continue beating until peaks start to form. Beat in sugar, 1 tablespoon at a time, then beat in vanilla. Spread meringue over filling and seal edges. Bake for 12 to 14 minutes. Cool before serving.

Joy Binnell
Upland, California
L.A. County Fair

 # Macadamia Nut Pie

1 baked 10-inch pie shell

Filling: **1 jar (3½ ounces) macadamia nuts,
preferably unsalted
½ cup sugar
1 envelope unflavored gelatin
2 tablespoons cornstarch
¼ teaspoon salt
1 package (3 ounces) cream cheese, softened
¼ cup sour cream
1½ cups milk
2 eggs, separated
4 tablespoons dark rum
1 cup heavy cream**

Preheat oven to 350°F.

If macadamia nuts are salted, spread on towel and rub to remove as much salt as possible. Chop nuts and place in a single layer on a baking sheet. Toast about 5 minutes, or until golden brown. Set aside.

Combine sugar, gelatin, cornstarch, and salt in a blender. Add cream cheese and sour cream. Whirl, gradually adding milk, and continue blending until smooth. Place mixture in top of a double boiler and cook over gently boiling water until thick and smooth, stirring continuously, about 15 minutes. Whisk some of the mixture into egg yolks and return to pan, whisking as it continues to cook, about 3 minutes. Remove top of double boiler and set aside to cool slightly.

Whip egg whites until stiff peaks form. Stir rum into filling mixture. Fold in egg whites. Chill until thickened but not firm.

*Brenda Berndt
Farmer's Branch,
Texas
State Fair of Texas*

Whip cream until stiff and fold into filling along with half the toasted nuts. Pour into baked pie crust. Chill at least 2 hours. Sprinkle top with remaining nuts just before serving.

Oatmeal Pie

Tastes like pecan pie, and won top prize at the "bake your own thing" contest of the Ionia County Free Fair.

1 unbaked 9-inch pie shell

Filling: **¾ cup sugar**
¾ cup corn syrup (light or dark)
¾ cup oatmeal
½ cup shredded coconut
¼ pound butter or margarine, melted
2 eggs, well beaten

Preheat oven to 350°F.

Mix all ingredients together. Pour into unbaked pie shell. Bake for 45 to 50 minutes.

Carol Sisler
Orleans, Michigan
Ionia County Free Fair

Peach Pie I

Mrs. Thornburg got her blue-ribbon recipe for peach pie from her mother.

1 unbaked 9-inch pie shell with top crust

Filling: **1 teaspoon lemon juice**
½ teaspoon almond extract
5 cups sliced peaches
1 cup plus 1 teaspoon sugar
4 tablespoons flour
¾ teaspoon cinnamon
3 tablespoons butter
¼ cup heavy cream

Preheat oven to 425°F.

Add lemon juice and almond extract to peaches. Stir together 1 cup sugar, flour, and cinnamon. Add to peaches and mix well. Pour into unbaked pie shell and dot with butter. Cover with top crust, flute edges, and vent top. Brush top with cream and sprinkle 1 teaspoon sugar on it. Bake at 425°F for 10 minutes, then reduce oven heat to 350°F and bake 40 minutes longer.

Lucretia Thornburg
Lancaster,
California
Antelope
Valley Fair

Peach Pie II

1 unbaked 9-inch pie shell with top crust

Filling: 3½ cups (1 pound, 13 ounce can) drained
sliced peaches, ½ cup syrup reserved
1 cup sugar
¼ cup flour
½ teaspoon cinnamon
1 tablespoon butter

Preheat oven to 425°F.

In a saucepan, combine sugar, flour, cinnamon, and ½ cup syrup. Cook over medium heat, stirring constantly, until mixture thickens and boils. Pour over drained peaches and mix. Turn peaches into unbaked pie shell and dot with butter. Cover with top crust, flute edges, and vent top (or you may wish to cover with lattice top). Bake for 35 to 40 minutes.

Marcia L. Mitchell
Walla Walla,
Washington
Southeastern
Washington
State Fair

Grandma Hook's Peach Pie

This recipe is a family favorite and has won a blue ribbon at the Branch County 4-H Fair for sixteen-year-old Lisa Kaye Hook.

1 unbaked 9-inch pie shell with top crust

Filling: **3 cups sliced peaches**
¼ cup (heaping) cornstarch
½ cup sugar
¼ teaspoon cinnamon

Preheat oven to 425°F.

Mix filling ingredients together and pour into unbaked pie shell. Cover with top crust, flute edges, and vent top. Bake at 425°F for 15 minutes, then lower oven heat to 350°F and bake for 30 minutes longer, or until done.

Lisa Kaye Hook
Montgomery,
Michigan
Branch County
4-H Fair

Pat's Peach Pie

"I always receive compliments on my peach pie," writes Pat Harder. Try it, and you will, too.

1 unbaked 9-inch pie shell with top crust

Filling: **4 cups sliced fresh peaches**
1¼ cups sugar
¼ cup quick-cooking tapioca
1 tablespoon lemon juice
⅛ teaspoon nutmeg
2 tablespoons butter

Preheat oven to 450°F.

Mix peaches with sugar, tapioca, lemon juice, and nutmeg. Pour into unbaked pie shell. Dot with butter. Cover with top crust, flute edges, and vent top. Sprinkle with a little sugar. Bake at 450°F for 10 minutes, then lower oven heat to 350°F and bake for another 30 minutes, or until light brown.

Pat Harder
LaPorte, Indiana
LaPorte
County Fair

Peach Cream Pie

1 unbaked 9-inch pie shell with top crust

Filling: **4 cups sliced peaches**
¾ cup light brown sugar
2 tablespoons plus 2 teaspoons cornstarch
½ teaspoon plus ⅛ teaspoon almond flavoring
8 ounces cream cheese
⅓ cup granulated sugar
2 tablespoons chopped toasted almonds
1 tablespoon butter

Preheat oven to 450°F.

In a bowl, combine peaches, brown sugar, 2 tablespoons cornstarch, and ½ teaspoon almond flavoring. In another bowl, place cream cheese, granulated sugar, 2 teaspoons cornstarch, and ⅛ teaspoon almond flavoring. Blend until creamy; stir in almonds. Turn cream cheese mixture into unbaked pie shell and spread evenly. Cover with peaches. Dot with butter. Cover with top crust, flute edges, and vent top. Bake in 450°F oven for 15 minutes, then reduce oven heat to 400°F and bake 30 minutes longer.

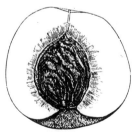

Tommie Arenas
Fresno, California
Fresno Fair

Peachy Peach Pie

"I made this recipe up," writes Mrs. Baker. "I wanted to use fruit of the season, something with color and good flavor." It won her first prize at the Erie County Fair.

1 unbaked 9-inch pie shell with pastry for
  a lattice crust

Filling: 4 cups sliced fresh peaches
1 teaspoon lemon juice
3 tablespoons quick-cooking tapioca
½ teaspoon cinnamon
⅔ cup sugar
½ cup flaked coconut
½ cup chopped maraschino cherries
2 tablespoons butter

Preheat oven to 425°F.

Sprinkle peaches with lemon juice. Add tapioca, cinnamon, and sugar and mix well. Fold in coconut and cherries and pour into pie shell. Dot with butter and top with lattice crust.

Bake for 30 to 35 minutes, or until crust is golden brown. Let cool and make topping:

Topping: 4 tablespoons confectioners' sugar
1½ tablespoons water

Mix together and drizzle on top of pie.

Mrs. DyAnn Baker
Hamburg,
New York
Erie County Fair

Peachy Raisin Nut Pie

1 unbaked 9-inch pie shell with top crust

Filling: **1 cup sugar**
½ teaspoon cinnamon
2½ tablespoons quick-cooking tapioca
4 cups sliced firm peaches
½ cup raisins
¾ cup chopped walnuts
1½ tablespoons butter

Preheat oven to 425°F.

Mix sugar, cinnamon, and tapioca in a bowl. Add peaches, raisins, and walnuts and toss to mix well. Turn filling into unbaked pie shell. Dot with butter. Cover with top crust, flute edges, and vent top. Bake for 35 to 45 minutes.

Maryanne
Goshgarian
Fresno, California
Fresno Fair

Peanut Butter Chiffon Pie

1 9-inch graham cracker crust
(Graham Cracker Crust I, page 24)

Filling: 1 envelope unflavored gelatin
½ cup boiling water
8 ounces cream cheese, softened
1 cup confectioners' sugar
⅓ cup smooth peanut butter
1 container (8 to 9 ounces) prepared
 nondairy whipped topping
¼ cup finely chopped peanuts

Dissolve gelatin in boiling water. Cool to luke-warm. Whip cream cheese until soft and fluffy. Beat in sugar and peanut butter. Slowly add gelatin mixture, blending thoroughly. Fold nondairy whipped topping into mixture. Pour into prepared pie shell. Sprinkle with peanuts. Chill for about 2 hours, or until firm.

Lois Auernheimer
Fresno, California
Fresno Fair

Pear Crumble Pie

1 unbaked 9-inch pie shell

Filling: 4 cups peeled and cored pears cut in eighths
1 teaspoon grated lemon rind
1 cup sugar
3 tablespoons lemon juice
½ cup flour
½ teaspoon ginger
¼ teaspoon mace
½ teaspoon cinnamon
5⅓ tablespoons butter or margarine

Preheat oven to 400°F.

Mix pears, lemon rind, ½ cup sugar, and lemon juice and arrange in unbaked pie shell. Combine flour, remaining ½ cup sugar, and spices. Cut butter into flour mixture until crumbly. Sprinkle over pears. Bake for about 45 minutes, or until pears are tender. Serve warm with whipped cream.

Dorothy Watts
Rantoul, Illinois
Champaign County Fair

 # Honey-Raisin Pear Pie

1 unbaked 9-inch pie shell, with pastry for
lattice crust

Filling: 1½ cups seedless raisins
1½ cups water
2 tablespoons cornstarch
⅔ cup honey
½ teaspoon nutmeg
2 teaspoons grated candied orange peel
1 tablespoon butter
2 medium-size Bartlett pears

Preheat oven to 350°F.

Place raisins and water in a saucepan. Bring to a boil, then turn down heat and simmer for 5 minutes. Mix cornstarch with a little water and blend into simmering raisins. Add honey and cook, stirring, until mixture is thickened and clear. Remove from heat and stir in nutmeg, grated orange peel, and butter. While mixture is cooling, pare, core, and slice the pears.

Pour half of raisin mixture into unbaked pie shell. Arrange pear slices on top, and pour rest of raisin mixture over the pear slices. Top with lattice crust and bake for 30 to 35 minutes, or until pears are tender when tested with a toothpick.

Arleen Owen
Fresno, California
Fresno Fair

Pecan Pie I

1 unbaked 9-inch pie shell

Filling: 4 eggs
1 cup sugar
½ cup light corn syrup
4 tablespoons butter or margarine,
    at room temperature
1 teaspoon vanilla extract
1 teaspoon butternut flavoring* (optional)
1 cup chopped pecans, or more

Preheat oven to 350°F.

Beat eggs slightly in a 2-quart bowl, mix in sugar, then corn syrup, butter or margarine, vanilla and butternut flavoring, and pecans. Pour into unbaked pie shell. Bake for 35 to 40 minutes, or until filling is slightly firm. Center of pie may look soft when pie is gently shaken, but it will become firm when cool.

Butternut flavoring can be ordered from:
Blair Products
1000 Robin's Road
Lynchburg, Virginia 24506
(804) 846-0028

Mrs. Johanna
Hodges
West Monroe,
Louisiana
Ark-La-Miss Fair

Pecan Pie II

Laura Turner is nineteen years old, loves to bake, and has been entering foods in the Montana Winter Fair since she was nine years old. She writes, "Once you win a ribbon it becomes an obsession and you're hooked." She has won many blue ribbons, one of them for her pecan pie.

1 unbaked 9-inch pie shell

Filling: **1 cup light corn syrup**
1 cup dark brown sugar
⅓ teaspoon salt
5⅓ tablespoons butter, melted
1 teaspoon vanilla extract
3 eggs
¾ cup chopped pecans
Whole pecans, for top of pie

Preheat oven to 350°F.
Combine all the ingredients except the whole pecans. Mix well. Pour into unbaked pie shell. Bake for 35 minutes. Remove pie briefly and arrange whole pecans on top. Bake 10 minutes longer, or until filling is set. Cool on rack.

Laura Turner
Bozeman, Montana
Montana
Winter Fair

Pecan-Rum Pumpkin Pie

1 baked 9-inch pie shell (Mostly Butter
Pie Crust, page 12)

Honey Pecans
for Garnish:
1 cup pecan halves
¼ cup honey
¾ cup water
3 tablespoons sugar
1 cup vegetable or peanut oil

In a saucepan, combine pecans, honey, and water,
and boil for 5 minutes. Drain pecans and return
them to the empty saucepan. Sprinkle with sugar
and toss over medium heat for 1 minute. Remove
from heat and continue tossing pecans with sugar
until they are evenly coated. Dry pecans on wax
paper for 15 minutes.

Heat oil to 375°F and deep-fry pecans for 2 minutes. Remove with a slotted spoon and dry on linen
(not paper) towel.

Filling:
1 cup pecans, coarsely chopped
½ cup plus ⅔ cup packed light brown sugar
3 tablespoons butter, at room temperature
1 cup evaporated milk
1 teaspoon cinnamon
½ teaspoon salt
¼ teaspoon cloves
¼ teaspoon nutmeg
1 cup cooked pumpkin (canned is O.K.)
2 eggs
3 tablespoons dark rum
½ teaspoon ginger

Preheat oven to 450°F.

Mix chopped nuts, ½ cup brown sugar, and butter; spread in bottom of pie crust. Blend milk with cinnamon, salt, cloves, and nutmeg. Mix pumpkin with eggs, ⅔ cup brown sugar, rum, and ginger. Then mix together with milk and spices. Carefully spoon filling into baked pie crust. Bake 10 minutes at 450°F, then reduce oven heat to 350°F and bake for 35 to 45 minutes longer, or until filling is set. Let cool completely. Garnish with sugar frosting and pecan halves.

Sugar Frosting Garnish:
4 tablespoons butter
2 tablespoons rum
Confectioners' sugar

Beat butter with rum; add enough confectioners' sugar to make a stiff icing of piping consistency.

Note: You may use whipped cream in place of icing.

Jaymi Sandler
Anchorage, Alaska
Anchorage Fur
Rendezvous

Finger Pecan Tarts

These delicious individual pecan tarts will delight your family and friends, as they have the Schroeder family for many generations.

Pastry: **3 ounces cream cheese**
¼ pound butter
1 cup flour

Mix cream cheese, butter, and flour together with a pastry blender. Roll into 24 balls the size of a large marble and press into small 1¾-inch cupcake tins.

Filling: **1½ cups light brown sugar**
2 tablespoons butter, melted
Pinch of salt (optional)
1 teaspoon vanilla extract
2 eggs, slightly beaten
1 cup chopped pecans

Preheat oven to 350°F.

In a pitcher, mix together sugar, butter, salt, vanilla, and eggs; pour into shells and top with nuts. Bake for 20 minutes, or until crusts turn golden and centers are firm.

Letitia E. Schroeder
Jackson,
Pennsylvania
Harford Fair

Pineapple Pie

1 unbaked 10-inch pie shell

Filling: ¼ pound butter
¾ cup sugar
4 egg yolks
1 large can (1 pound, 13 ounces) crushed
  pineapple, drained, with juice reserved
2 egg whites (save other two for meringue)

Meringue: 2 egg whites
¼ teaspoon cream of tartar
4 tablespoons confectioners' sugar
½ teaspoon vanilla extract

Preheat oven to 350°F.

Cream butter and sugar together. Add egg yolks and mix well. Add drained pineapple and 3 tablespoons of the juice. Beat the 2 egg whites until stiff, and fold into egg yolk mixture. Pour into unbaked pie shell and bake for 30 minutes, or until filling is set.

Make meringue. Beat egg whites until frothy. Add cream of tartar and continue beating until peaks are formed. Beat in sugar, 1 tablespoon at a time, then beat in vanilla. Cover pie with meringue and bake 10 to 15 minutes longer.

Mrs. H.V. Parsons
West Monroe,
Louisiana
Louisiana State Fair

Plum Pie

1 unbaked 9-inch pie shell with top crust

Filling: 3½ cups peeled, pitted, and sliced plums, peels reserved
2½ tablespoons quick-cooking tapioca
4 thin slices lemon with the rind
1 cup plus 1 teaspoon sugar
¼ teaspoon allspice
1 tablespoon butter
1 egg white
1 tablespoon water

Preheat oven to 425°F.

Purée the reserved plum peels in a food processor or blender. Add to plums along with tapioca. Mix well and let stand for 15 minutes. Quarter the lemon slices and add them to the plums, along with 1 cup sugar and allspice. Mix well and turn into unbaked pie shell. Dot with butter. Cover with top crust, flute edges, and prick top of crust with a fork. Beat egg white with water and brush over top crust. Sprinkle with 1 teaspoon sugar. Bake at 425°F for 10 minutes, then reduce oven heat to 375°F and continue baking for 35 minutes longer.

Tommie Arenas
Fresno, California
Fresno Fair

French Plum Pie
with Crumb Topping

1 unbaked 9-inch pie shell

Filling: ⅓ cup sugar
½ teaspoon cinnamon
4 tablespoons flour
4 cups peeled, pitted, and sliced plums
(Santa Rosa or other available plums)

Crumb 6 tablespoons butter or margarine
Topping: 6 tablespoons brown sugar
¾ cup flour

Preheat oven to 400°F.

Mix sugar, cinnamon, and flour together. Toss with plums. Turn plums into unbaked pie shell.

Blend butter, brown sugar, and flour together and sprinkle over plums. Bake for 35 to 40 minutes.

Marge Ohanesian
Fresno, California
Fresno Fair

Pumpkin Pie

1 unbaked 9-inch pie shell

Filling: 2 cups mashed cooked pumpkin
2 tablespoons butter or margarine
3 eggs, beaten
¾ cup sugar
2 tablespoons flour
½ teaspoon salt
1 teaspoon cinnamon
½ teaspoon cloves
¼ teaspoon ginger
½ cup shredded coconut
½ cup evaporated milk

Preheat oven to 400°F.
Combine all the filling ingredients and mix well. Pour into unbaked pie shell and bake at 400°F for 15 minutes, then reduce oven heat to 350°F and bake for 45 minutes longer. Cool on rack. Top with whipped cream or Cool Whip, if desired, just before serving.

Betty Joyce Rhodes
Brandon, Mississippi
Harvest Festival
at Mississippi
Agriculture and
Forestry Museum

Walnut-Glazed Pumpkin Pie

A large rectangular pie for a crowd of happy eaters.

Unbaked double-crust Basic Pie Crust (page 11)

Shape pastry into a ball and roll out into a rectangle. Pat pastry into bottom and up sides of a 13 × 9-inch baking pan. Flute edges.
Preheat oven to 400°F.

Filling: 1 can (29 ounces) pumpkin purée
2 cups evaporated milk
½ cup sugar
½ cup packed light brown sugar
5 eggs
¼ teaspoon salt
1 teaspoon nutmeg
¼ teaspoon cloves
1 teaspoon ginger
4 teaspoons cinnamon

In a large bowl, combine pumpkin, evaporated milk, white and brown sugar, and eggs. Beat with a wire whisk or hand beater until well mixed, then beat in salt and all the spices. Pour filling into pie crust. Bake for 45 minutes, or until knife inserted into center comes out clean.

Glazed-Walnut Topping: 2 cups chopped walnuts
½ cup dark corn syrup

Cook walnuts in a cast-iron skillet over medium heat, stirring frequently, until lightly browned. Remove from heat and stir in corn syrup to mix well. Gently spread walnut mixture evenly over top of pie. Cover and refrigerate.

Carolyn Lincoln
Madera, California
Madera
District Fair

Pumpkin Cheese Pie

This delicious variation on the classic pumpkin pie won first prize at the Wisconsin State Fair. These pies are best prepared the day before serving.

2 unbaked 9-inch pie shells

Filling:
3 cups pumpkin purée (fresh or canned)
1 cup firmly packed light brown sugar
1½ teaspoons cinnamon
1½ teaspoons ginger
¾ teaspoon nutmeg
¾ teaspoon cloves
3 eggs, slightly beaten
1½ cups evaporated milk
1½ teaspoons vanilla extract

Preheat oven to 350°F.
Combine all filling ingredients in large bowl of electric mixer. Beat well. Divide between the two pie shells.

Cheese Topping:
12 ounces cream cheese, softened
¾ cup sugar
3 eggs, slightly beaten
1½ teaspoons vanilla extract

Combine all topping ingredients in small bowl of electric mixer. Beat until smooth. Spoon the mixture carefully over the pumpkin filling, dividing topping between the two pies.
Bake for 50 to 60 minutes, or until knife inserted in center comes out clean. Cool on racks. Chill for 24 hours before serving.

Ursula Maurer
Wauwatosa, Illinois
Wisconsin
State Fair

Old-Fashioned Raisin Pie

The Rev. Floyd T. Robinson sent his wife's family recipe that won him first prize at the Kentucky State Fair.

1 unbaked 9-inch pie shell with top crust or lattice

Filling:
2 cups raisins
2 cups water
½ cup packed light brown sugar
2 tablespoons cornstarch
½ teaspoon cinnamon
¼ teaspoon salt
1 tablespoon vinegar
1 tablespoon butter or margarine

Preheat oven to 425°F.

Combine raisins and water in a saucepan and boil for 5 minutes. Mix together sugar, cornstarch, cinnamon, and salt. Add to raisins and cook, stirring, until liquid is clear. Remove from heat. Stir in vinegar and butter and cool slightly.

Pour into unbaked pie shell, cover with top pastry or lattice strips, and bake about 30 minutes, or until top is golden brown.

Rev. Floyd T.
Robinson
Louisville,
Kentucky
Kentucky State Fair

Cider Raisin Pie

1 unbaked 9-inch pie shell with top crust

Filling: 1½ cups water
15 ounces dark raisins
1½ cups apple cider
¾ cup sugar
1 cup chunky applesauce (unsweetened)
1 teaspoon salt
1 teaspoon cinnamon
¼ cup lemon juice
3 tablespoons butter
3 tablespoons cornstarch

Preheat oven to 425°F.

Combine 1 cup water with raisins, cider, sugar, applesauce, salt, cinnamon, lemon juice, and butter in a saucepan. Heat to a boil. Mix cornstarch with remaining ½ cup water. Stir into hot mixture and cook, stirring, until thick. Cool slightly.

Pour into unbaked pie shell. Cover with top crust, flute edges, and vent top. Bake at 425°F for 15 minutes, then reduce oven heat to 350°F and bake for 35 minutes longer. Cool completely before cutting.

Mrs. William A.
Woods
Spring Hill, Florida
Florida State Fair

Cranberry-Raisin Pie

1 unbaked 9-inch pie shell, with pastry for
lattice crust

Filling: 1 cup light brown sugar
2 tablespoons cornstarch
2 cups raisins
½ teaspoon freshly diced orange peel
½ cup orange juice
½ teaspoon finely diced lemon peel
2 tablespoons lemon juice
1⅓ cups cold water
1 cup cranberries

Preheat oven to 375°F.

Combine brown sugar and cornstarch in a saucepan. Stir in raisins, orange peel and juice, lemon peel and juice, and cold water. Cook and stir over medium heat until thick and bubbly, then cook, stirring, 1 minute longer. Remove from heat and stir in cranberries. Let cool a little, then pour into unbaked pie shell. Top with lattice crust. Bake for 40 minutes.

Susan Garner
Fresno, California
Fresno Fair

 # Sour Cream Raisin Pie

This scrumptious raisin pie is topped off with an unusual brown-sugar meringue.

1 baked 9-inch pie shell

Filling: **1½ tablespoons cornstarch**
1 cup plus 2 tablespoons sugar
¼ teaspoon salt
¾ teaspoon nutmeg
1½ cups sour cream
3 egg yolks
1½ cups raisins
1 tablespoon lemon juice

Combine cornstarch, sugar, salt, and nutmeg in a saucepan. Blend in the sour cream, then the egg yolks, raisins, and lemon juice. Cook over medium heat, stirring constantly, until mixture is thick and comes to a boil. Boil 1 minute and turn into baked pie shell. Prepare meringue.

Brown-Sugar Meringue: **3 egg whites, at room temperature**
¼ teaspoon cream of tartar
6 tablespoons brown sugar
½ teaspoon vanilla extract

Preheat oven to 400°F.
Whip egg whites until frothy. Beat in cream of tartar and continue beating until peaks start to form. Beat in sugar, 1 tablespoon at a time, then beat in vanilla. Heap meringue onto pie and seal edges. Bake for 10 minutes. Let cool away from drafts.

Mrs. Marian Potts
St. Paul, Nebraska
Howard
County Fair

 # Walnut Raisin Pie

1 unbaked 9-inch pie shell

Filling: ¾ cup sugar
2 tablespoons cornstarch
¼ teaspoon nutmeg
¼ teaspoon cloves
½ teaspoon cinnamon
Dash of salt
2 cups cranberry-apple juice
2 cups raisins
½ teaspoon black-walnut extract (optional)

Topping: ½ cup packed light brown sugar
⅓ cup flour
4 tablespoons butter, softened
½ cup finely chopped walnuts

Preheat oven to 450°F.

In a large saucepan, combine sugar, cornstarch, nutmeg, cloves, cinnamon, and salt. Blend in cranberry-apple juice. Add raisins and cook over low heat, stirring constantly, until thick and clear. Add black-walnut extract. Cool slightly. Turn into unbaked pie shell.

Prepare topping: Mix brown sugar with flour. Cut in butter until crumbly. Add walnuts. Sprinkle topping evenly over pie filling. Bake at 450°F for 10 minutes, then reduce oven heat to 350°F and continue to bake 20 minutes longer, or until pastry is golden brown.

Carolyn Lincoln
Madera, California
Madera
District Fair

Red Raspberry Pie

The crisp sugar crust of this mouth-watering pie is filled with shimmering red raspberries. It won a blue ribbon as well as first place in the fruit-pie-of-the-day competition at the Illinois State Fair.

1 baked 8- or 9-inch pie shell
  (Sugar Pie Crust, page 22)

Filling: **1 cup sugar**
       1 cup water
       3 tablespoons cornstarch
       3 tablespoons raspberry Jell-O (dry)
       1½ quarts red raspberries

Combine sugar, water, and cornstarch in a saucepan. Cook, stirring, until thickened and clear. Add the Jell-O and mix well. Arrange raspberries in bottom of baked pie shell. Pour Jell-O syrup over berries, making sure all are covered. Refrigerate until thoroughly cooled. Garnish with whipped cream, if desired.

Jane E. Hurshma
Springfield, Illinois
Illinois State Fair

Raspberry-Apple Pie

1 unbaked 9-inch pie shell with top crust

Filling: 2 cups peeled, sliced apples
¼ cup apple juice, or other fruit juice
2 cups raspberries
¾ cup sugar
3 tablespoons cornstarch
1 teaspoon nutmeg

Preheat oven to 450°F.

In a saucepan, combine apple slices with apple juice and steam, covered, for a few minutes until the apples begin to soften. Remove and let cool slightly. Mix apples with raspberries. Mix sugar, cornstarch, and nutmeg and mix with berry-apple mixture. Turn into unbaked pie shell. Cover with top crust, flute edges, and vent top. Bake at 450°F for 15 minutes, then reduce oven heat to 350°F and bake 30 minutes longer.

Margie Storelli
Fresno, California
Fresno Fair

Rhubarb Pie I

Norma Fenn has won seventeen blue ribbons in ten years for her pies. Try her original recipe for rhubarb pie and you'll know why it's a winner.

1 unbaked 9-inch pie shell with top crust (Pastry Mix, page 20)

Filling: **1 cup sugar**
1 small package strawberry Jell-O
3 cups chopped rhubarb

Preheat oven to 350°F.

Mix sugar and Jell-O together and add to rhubarb. Mix well and pour into pie shell. Cover with top crust, seal the edges, and cut a few slits with a sharp knife to let out steam. Bake for 45 to 50 minutes. Cool and refrigerate before serving.

Norma Fenn
Roseburg, Oregon
Douglas
County Fair

Rhubarb Pie II

Sister Concepta Marie Nudo of Immaculate Conception Convent has won many blue ribbons for her baking. Her rhubarb pie was awarded the Grand Championship at the Heart of Illinois Fair.

**1 unbaked 10-inch pie shell with top crust
(Pie Crust with Margarine and Lard, page 14)**

Filling: **1 cup sugar
3 tablespoons flour
Pinch of salt
¾ teaspoon Fruit Fresh* (optional)
2 cups diced rhubarb
Few drops of red food coloring (optional,
     but makes it look nice)
1 tablespoon margarine
¼ cup sugar
¼ cup milk**

Preheat oven to 400°F.

Combine sugar, flour, salt, and Fruit Fresh. Mix with diced rhubarb. Add a few drops of red food coloring and stir well. Turn into unbaked pie shell and dot with margarine. Cover with top crust and flute edges. Mix sugar and milk together and brush top of pie crust. Just before putting into oven, prick top crust with a fork in several places to vent. Bake for 40 to 45 minutes, or until golden brown.

*Ascorbic acid.

*Sister Concepta
Marie Nudo
Peoria, Illinois
Heart of
Illinois Fair*

Rhubarb Custard Pie

1 unbaked 9-inch pie shell, with pastry for
lattice crust

Filling: 3 eggs
1½ cups sugar
2 tablespoons flour
1 tablespoon orange juice
¼ teaspoon grated orange rind
2 cups diced rhubarb

Preheat oven to 450°F.

Beat eggs slightly, then mix in sugar, flour, orange juice, and rind. Add rhubarb, mix well, and pour into unbaked pie shell. Top with lattice crust. Place pie in oven and reduce heat to 350°F. Bake 40 minutes, or until custard is set and browned.

*Maurine L. Saunders
Longview,
Washington
Cowlitz
County Fair*

Spaghetti Squash-Coconut Pie

1 baked 9-inch pie shell

Filling: 4 tablespoons margarine
3 tablespoons flour
1¼ cups sugar
1½ cups milk
3 egg yolks, well beaten
1 cup cooked spaghetti squash (well drained)
1 teaspoon coconut flavoring

Meringue: 3 egg whites
½ teaspoon cream of tartar
6 tablespoons sugar

Preheat oven to 350°F.

Melt the margarine in a heavy saucepan. Stir in flour, sugar, and milk. Cook, stirring, until thickened. Beat some of hot mixture into egg yolks, and when they are warmed, gradually stir them into hot mixture. Cook, stirring, for 1 or 2 minutes more. Stir in spaghetti squash and coconut flavoring. Remove from heat and let cool. Turn into baked pie shell.

Prepare meringue: Whip egg whites until frothy. Beat in cream of tartar and continue beating until peaks start to form. Beat in sugar, 1 tablespoon at a time, and continue beating until stiff peaks form. Spread meringue on pie and bake for 15 to 20 minutes, or until browned.

Methyl Grissom
Leighton, Alabama
North Alabama
State Fair

Pat's Strawberry Pie

1 unbaked 9-inch pie shell with top crust

Filling: 1 quart strawberries
1 cup plus 1 teaspoon sugar
3 tablespoons quick-cooking tapioca
2 tablespoons butter

Preheat oven to 450°F.

Remove stems from berries and slice them in half or thirds, depending on size. Mix berries with 1 cup sugar and tapioca. Pour into unbaked pie shell. Dot with butter. Cover with top crust, flute edges, and vent top. Sprinkle top crust with 1 teaspoon sugar and bake at 450°F for 10 minutes, then lower oven heat to 350°F and bake for 30 minutes longer, or until light brown.

Pat Harder
LaPorte, Indiana
LaPorte
County Fair

Strawberry Cream Pie

1 baked 8- or 9-inch pie shell

Filling: ⅔ cup sugar
½ cup flour
½ teaspoon salt
2 cups milk, scalded
2 eggs, separated
2 tablespoons butter
1 teaspoon vanilla extract
1 quart fresh strawberries, hulled and sliced
1 cup confectioners' sugar

Mix sugar, flour, and salt together and dissolve with some of the hot milk. Gradually blend wih the rest of the hot milk. Cook over low heat until mixture thickens, stirring constantly. Beat egg yolks in a bowl. Stir a small amount of hot mixture into egg yolks; stir warmed egg yolks into hot mixture. Cook over low heat for 1 minute longer. Remove from heat and stir in butter and vanilla. Let cool.

Reserve 1 cup of strawberries. Place remaining strawberries in pie shell. Spread cooled custard over top. Beat egg whites and confectioners' sugar, a little at a time, until stiff. Fold in reserved berries. Spread over top of pie. Refrigerate until ready to serve.

Judith See
Monroe, Michigan
Michigan 4-H

Strawberry-Rhubarb Pie I

1 unbaked 9-inch pie shell, with pastry for
lattice top

Filling: 4 cups sliced rhubarb
2 cups sliced strawberries
1½ cups sugar
4 tablespoons flour
Pinch of salt
1 tablespoon butter

Preheat oven to 425°F.
Combine rhubarb, strawberries, sugar, flour, and
salt. Turn into unbaked pie shell. Dot with butter
and cover with pastry strips to make a lattice top.
Bake 10 minutes at 425°F, then reduce oven heat to
350°F and bake 30 minutes longer.

Mary Gail Alesse
Sandwich,
Massachusetts
Barnstable
County Fair

Strawberry-Rhubarb Pie II

1 unbaked 9-inch pie shell with top crust

Filling: 2 cups sliced strawberries
2 cups sliced rhubarb
1 cup sugar
¼ cup strawberry Jell-O
3 tablespoons quick-cooking tapioca

Preheat oven to 375°F.

Mix together strawberries, rhubarb, sugar, Jell-O, and tapioca. Turn into unbaked pie shell. Cover with top crust, flute edges, and vent top. Bake for 40 minutes, or until pie is brown and bubbly.

Amelia Rosenberry
Abingdon, Illinois
Knox County Fair

Sweet Potato Pie

1 baked 9-inch pie shell

Filling: 4 medium-size sweet potatoes, boiled and mashed
4 egg yolks
2 cups sugar
1 teaspoon cinnamon
½ cup vegetable shortening

Topping: ¼ to ½ cup butter-flavored Crisco shortening
1 cup confectioners' sugar
1 teaspoon vanilla extract
Pinch of baking powder

Preheat oven to 350°F.

Combine potatoes, egg yolks, sugar, and cinnamon and blend with a mixer. Blend in shortening. Pour into baked pie shell. Bake 15 to 20 minutes.

Prepare topping: Blend shortening, sugar, and vanilla with mixer until fluffy. Blend in baking powder (this keeps the topping in peaks). Arrange over top of warm pie. Bake in 350°F oven until browned.

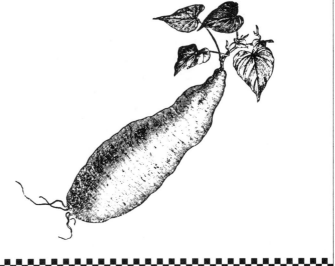

Leslie Stafford
Sheffield, Alabama
North Alabama
State Fair

Zucchini Pie

This dessert tastes like apple crisp and will fool your family.

Pie Crust: 4 cups flour
2 cups sugar
½ teaspoon salt
¾ pound margarine

Filling: 6 to 8 cups seeded, peeled, and sliced zucchini
⅔ cup lemon juice
1 cup sugar
¼ teaspoon nutmeg
1½ teaspoons cinnamon

Preheat oven to 375°F.

Prepare the pastry: Combine flour, sugar, and salt in a bowl. Cut in margarine until crumbly. Press half the mixture over the bottom of a greased 9 × 13-inch baking pan. Reserve remaining pastry mixture. Bake for 10 minutes. Remove and set aside.

In a saucepan, cook zucchini in lemon juice until tender, about 10 minutes. Add sugar, nutmeg, and 1 teaspoon cinnamon. Simmer for 1 minute. Stir in ½ cup reserved pastry mixture. Simmer until mixture thickens, stirring constantly. Let cool.

Pour zucchini mixture over crust. Mix ½ teaspoon cinnamon with remaining pastry mixture in bowl. Sprinkle over pie. Bake for 35 to 45 minutes, or until lightly browned.

Doris Burns
Washtenaw,
Michigan

Pam Pistor
Lenawee, Michigan
Michigan 4-H

Resources

Readers who are interested in regional or specialty cookbooks may purchase them by mail from the following organizations:

Blue Ribbon Baked Goods
Anchorage Fur Rendezvous
P.O. Box 773
Anchorage, Alaska 99510

Award Winning Recipes
L.A. County Fair
P.O. Box 2250
Pomona, California 91769

Prize Winners Plus Cookbook
State Fair of Oklahoma
P.O. Box 74943
Oklahoma City, Oklahoma 73147

Prize Winning Recipes
State Fair of Texas
P.O. Box 26010
Dallas, Texas 75226

Savor It!
Michigan 4-H Foundation
1407 South Harrison Avenue
East Lansing, Michigan 48823

Index

Lee, Nancy, 75
Leigh, Ellen, 72
Lemon Buttermilk Pie, Southern, 76
Lemon Cake Pie, 77
lemon filling, for Angel Pie, 32
Lemon-Lime Daiquiri Pie, 78–79
Lemon Meringue Pie, 71–72
Lemon Pie, Best-Ever, 73–74
Lemon Sponge Pie, Aunt Dolly's, 75
Lime Daiquiri Pie, Lemon-, 78–79
Lime Meringue Pie, 80
Lincoln, Carolyn, 102, 108
Linda's Apple Pie, 34
lining, pie plate, 5–6
Luke's Cherry Pie, 56
Lynn, Kristie, 58

M

Macadamia Nut Pie, 81
Margarine and Lard, Pie Crust with, 13, 14
Margarine Pastry, 13
    for Old-Fashioned Blueberry Pie, 45
Maurer, Ursula, 103
McAlister, Joy, 62
meringue
    for Apricot Pie, 38
    for Best-Ever Lemon Pie, 73
    for Blackberry Jam Pie, 43
    Brown Sugar, for Sour Cream Raisin Pie, 107

meringue (*continued*)
    for Buttermilk Raisin Pie, 50
    for Butterscotch Pie, 51
    crust, for Angel Pie, 32
    for Lemon Meringue Pie, 71
    for Lime Meringue Pie, 80
    Never-Fail, 73
    for Pineapple Pie, 98
    for Spaghetti Squash-Coconut Pie, 114
    temperature of ingredients for, 7
Meringue Pie
    Lemon, 71–72
    Lime, 80
microwave oven, 63
Mishler, Esther, 54
Mitchell, Joyce, 57
Mitchell, Marcia L., 84
mixing pie pastry, 4–5
Mostly Butter Pie Crust, 12
    for Pecan Rum Pumpkin Pie, 95–96

N

Never-Fail Meringue, 73
Never-Fail Pie Crust, 16
    for Apple Custard Pie, 36
Niccum, Nikki, 44
Nudo, Sister Concepta Marie, 14, 112
Nut Pie
    Macadamia, 81
    Peachy Raisin, 89
Nutty Chocolate Pie Dough, 23